The Art of the 'Ask'

A collection of fundraising letters and telephone scripts

Connie S. Pheiff

The Art of the Ask: A collection of fundraising letters and telephone Scripts

ISBN: 978-0-9893202-1-4
Published by Dragonfly Press
Printed in the United States of America
2013

For information about custom editions, special sales, premium and corporate purchases, please contact Dragonfly Press Sales Department at 570.906.4395 or info@conniepheiffspeaks.com.

Dedication

To my former employers…
You gave me the entrepreneurial strength to share my wisdom
and courage through my speaking, coaching, and writing.

Author's Note

I wrote this book to help nonprofit staff and experienced fundraising professionals excel in today's tough fundraising environment. The nonprofit sector continues to be ravaged by changes—everything from scandals to the realignment of borders of national organizations. No matter what level you are in the organization, the information in this book will help you understand that Attitude + Passion = Results (A+P=R), and determine if you have the right attitude to be working in the nonprofit sector.

The *Art of the Ask* is actually quite simple:

- You make your ask.
- You make your case.
- You show the benefits.
- Then you stop talking.

The teachings and stories in this book can be read from different perspectives: current executive directors, aspiring executive directors, development officers, board members, and community stakeholders.

Whether the organization you work for is large or small, this book gives you the tools to determine if you are in the right place in your career. "Large" is the equivalent of state and national NPOs. "Small" is the equivalent of an organization that does not carry a charter from big brother. In the end, all NPOs need to have a local presence with grassroots efforts. Donors need to know, like, and respect you. Unfortunately, organizations are looking at the economies of scale and closing local offices. This, in my opinion, negatively affects the organization's fundraising efforts.

Philanthropy giving is not disappearing. Giving simply looks different these days, and we need to be open to the ways of work. With change come new opportunities. The big change we're realizing is that the world is much more flat and connected than we ever thought possible. This means you have greater opportunities to increase your fundraising efforts.

Do you have the tools necessary to fundraise in your toolbox? I have been fundraising for years and have written telephone scripts and a letter or two or three... The telephone scripts and letters include getting the appointment, annual giving, special events, volunteer recruitment, sustainability, overdue pledges, and commitment. The letters in this book is just another element for your fundraising war chest.

Contents

Foreword   11

Introduction   15

Chapter 1
What is Fundraising?   19

Chapter 2
Overcoming Objections   21

Chapter 3
Basic Telephone Scripts   29

Chapter 4
Membership Letters   39

Chapter 5
Membership Telephone Scripts   45

Chapter 6
Personal Touch   51

Chapter 7   57
Get Donors to Call You!

Chapter 8   61
What to Say to Donors…and What Not to Say

Chapter 9   65
Go for the 'ask!'

Chapter 10   69
Fundraising Letters

Chapter 11   77
Fundraising Telephone Track

Chapter 12
Did You Say – Sponsorship?   83

Chapter 13
Sponsorship Telephone Track   93

Chapter 14
Get Your Board on Board!   97

Chapter 15
Sponsorship Examples   107

Chapter 16
Pledge Reminder/Overdue Letter   113

Chapter 17
Stay The Course   115

Chapter 18
The '4' Biggest Mistakes a Fundraiser Makes   117

Chapter 19
Make Yourself Standout   121

Tips | Recommended Reading | Resources   127

About the Author   131

What others are Saying   137

"Remember the words of the Lord Jesus, how he said, it is more blessed to give than to receive."
~Acts 20:35

"We make a living by what we get, but we make a life by what we give."
~Winston Churchill

"In the long run, we shape our lives, and we shape ourselves. The process never ends until we die. And the choices we make are ultimately our own responsibility".
~Eleanor Roosevelt

"Ignite your Passion."
~Connie S. Pheiff

Foreword

We've seen Jeff Skoll (eBay), Mark Zuckerberg (Facebook), Bill Gates (Microsoft), Warren Buffet (Berkshire Hathaway), Michael Bloomberg (New York City Mayor and founder of Bloomberg Financial News Service), and others commit to The Giving Pledge—pledging to give away at least half of their wealth to philanthropic causes. These individuals built for-profit businesses but then structured those profits to be plowed into worthy endeavors.

The key concept in understanding how to tap into these rich resources is not to simply raise your hand as a nonprofit organization. These wealthy donors are looking far beyond just the legal structure to the very things that allowed their businesses to be so successful. In the for-profit world, things like poor financial controls, inability to adapt, fierce competition, ineffective management, and technology and social media changes cause businesses to close or to be swallowed by similar organizations. Knowledgeable business leaders are quick to recognize similar challenges in nonprofit companies.

Innovative types of organizations are blurring the distinctions between for-profit and nonprofit entities. New terms like social entrepreneurship, ethical capitalism, and "B" corporations are emerging and showing their ability to address issues like pollution, poverty, and illiteracy that were historically only the domain of the nonprofit world. John Sage (Pura Vida Coffee), Tom Szaky (TerraCycle), Blake Mycoskie (TOMS Shoes), and many others are leading the way with for-profit businesses that are doing well while doing good. In today's economic workplace you can change the world, address poverty or pollution, make the world a better place … *and make money* in the process.

Bottom line: The legal structure of an organization is less important than having a worthy mission to fulfill, as well as a business structure that is efficient and compelling. Wealthy donors expect business excellence in the causes they choose to support.

As clarified in *The Art of the Ask*, "Fundraising is a business; it's not your mother's charity anymore." And the people in that business are the face and voice of it. Ultimately donor's give to people they know, like, and trust. You are selling an idea, a cause, a better way of life, or a solution to a recognized problem. In the world of selling we often tell people that true, professional selling is simply sharing enthusiasm. And fortunately, that enthusiasm can be enhanced by proper attitude and confidence, coupled with knowing when to be silent.

To compete in today's marketplace we have to compete on quality and value to earn the right to ask people to support our causes. We can't offer shoddy service, inefficient money management, substandard necklaces, or second-rate coffee and expect people to get excited about helping us in our worthy endeavors. We have to believe we are the very best. We have to be proud of what we are representing and then hold our heads high as we invite people to be part of something great. Our passion for what we are doing can then exceed any fear or sense of inadequacy.

You are reading a tool that will enhance your ability to do something great. *The Art of the Ask* provides the steps to standing above the crowd. The organization you represent deserves more than just adequate resources. You can tap into the rich resources of wealth waiting to be released into your care.

Being excellent at raising resources requires more than being part of a worthy organization. *The Art of the Ask* can put you in the top 5 percent of fundraising experts. This success, as in any area of life, is not luck. Rather, it's when preparation meets opportunity. Enjoy your *preparation.*

**~*Dan Miller, coach and author of*
48 Days to the Work You Love**

Introduction

You can do a simple Internet search and find many quotes about giving—many quotes that tell you the only thing that really matters is your attitude. After years of fundraising (too many to mention), I know this belief is true. *Your attitude is everything when it comes to fundraising.*

My fundraising initiatives began with the small PTA bake sales. Over time my passion for fundraising expanded, and eventually I was asking for big dollars for the Chamber of Commerce of the United States.

As a fundraiser and former employee of the nonprofit sector, I know how valuable your time can be. So let me get right to the point: **This book is a how-to for those who face fundraising with fear. It will show you how Attitude + Passion = Results (A + P = R)**

First, realize that if you fear fundraising then you are in the wrong position. When coaching executive directors, development officers, and board members, I find that most have a passion for the organization they represent. I also find that most have a fear of fundraising. In this book we will address why having the right people in the fundraising role, as well as having the right attitude, will make your fundraising efforts so much more productive.

I will not talk about the historical philosophies that surround fundraising. If you are like me, you have already listened to CDs, read fundraising books, and attended gobs of seminars to learn how to fundraise. In plain language I will provide examples of real world experience and what I recommend as the most valuable pieces of information you need to be a successful fundraiser.

My best fundraising efforts were with the Chamber of Commerce of the United States. My work was directly with the President of the Chamber and Senior Vice Presidents. Initially, I started as a telephone sales representative. (Hey, we all have to start somewhere, right?) I was quickly promoted to downtown Washington D.C., right across from the White House. I made it! I was working in the District! Honestly, this was one of the best times of my working career.

My position was to work with the executive team to develop a 16-month plan to revitalize the Chamber of Commerce of the United States. Here are the highlights.

I. Fix the infrastructure through finances and membership recruitment, and put retention systems in place.
II. Reorganize the membership system.
III. Enhance the commercial operations and partnerships.
IV. Strengthen relationships of state and local Chambers of Commerce, government officials, and the media.
V. Advance the core agenda.
VI. Defend businesses against attacks on the enterprise system.

Funding, in large amounts, needed to happen for these changes to take place. For nearly 18 months, a 40-city tour took place where we visited corridors of power in Washington, D.C. and across the country asking for BIG money.

Of course, that's just one example of my success. In this book I will share best practices in the industry—the ones I learned from my mentors as well as the ones I gleamed from the school of hard knocks. You'll learn how your attitude is the key to fundraising success (and how to change yours if you need to), as well as hands-on strategies that will make your fundraising efforts more prosperous.

You will see I answer questions that I hear from my coaching clients from the nonprofit sector. They may be questions you thought of, but afraid to ask.

Remember, a nonprofit is a business; it's not your mother's charity anymore. This book is not meant to simplify your existence, but to streamline your efforts. Refer to these pages time and time again, and you'll soon become the next fundraising superstar.

Chapter 1
What is Fundraising?

According to Webster's Dictionary, fundraising or fund raising (also development) is the process of soliciting and gathering voluntary contributions of money or other resources, by requesting donations from individuals, businesses, charitable foundations, or governmental agencies. Although fundraising typically refers to efforts to gather money for nonprofit organizations, it is sometimes used to refer to the identification and solicitation of investors or other sources of capital for for-profit enterprises.

Traditionally, fundraising consisted mostly of asking for donations on the street or at people's doors, such as selling Girl Scout cookies. These days, fundraising takes on many forms as social networking is emerging; however, grassroots fundraising continues to be the best method for increasing funds. From a direct "ask" for money to events and program sales, fundraising is a constant for a nonprofit organization.

Why is Fundraising Important?

Although an organization is called a "nonprofit," fundraising needs to include the cost of doing business. Today, a nonprofit is not your mother's charity; most are well-run machines.

The definition of a nonprofit is "not to profit." But if there was no profit, then how could the organization turn the lights on in the morning, pay staff salaries, conduct staff training, or hire a professional fundraiser? The cost of running a nonprofit can be enormous. Today, donors are keener on an organization's mission, and when making a donation they will designate the funds to go directly to a specific program. But again, the organization needs funds just to function, much less provide whatever program or service they offer.

For your nonprofit to be successful—and for you to be a successful fundraiser—you need to adopt a new two-word descriptor for what fundraising is all about. Those two words are:

1. Consistency – If you want your funders to return year after year, you and your organization must display consistency in your message and your tactics.
2. Attitude – Whether you're asking for a large amount or a small one, whether from an individual or a company, your confident attitude plays a huge role in how the donor responds.

Before we delve into the core information, please note that I don't know of any magic wand or secret formula. Fundraising is hard work. To be successful at it requires a consistent, persistent, determined, and intentional attitude when making "the ask." Now it's time to discover how to speak on the telephone to writing a fundraising letter that will take you to the bank. Organizations reflected are for sample purposes only.

To avoid situations in which you might make mistakes may be the biggest mistake of all.

~Peter McWilliams

Chapter 2
Overcome Objections

Sometimes, the donor will tell you "no." That's okay, because a "no" doesn't always mean "no." Often, a "no" is a "maybe" or a "tell me more" in disguise. The good news is that you can turn a "no" into a "yes."

We are talking about fundraising, but the same rules apply in sales positions. You will always have to be prepared to deal with the potential donors "objections." You should not be afraid of the objections as long as you are prepared.

You can find numerous books at your local library or bookstore on how to manage objection responses. Jeffrey Fox's book *How to be a Rainmaker* provides an effective method for managing objections. Jeffrey Gitomer, *The Salesman* is renowned for his sales training techniques. His mantra "people don't like to be sold, but they like to buy" is true. Even donors want to give to a worthy cause; it is up to you to help them determine how much they will give to your cause.

If you have been fundraising for a while you will know that rarely you will get your donor's acknowledgment on the first 'ask.' From my experience it typically takes at least seven 'ask' before getting your first 'yes.' Next time you are planning to meet with a potential donor have your list of objection responses prepared. Order pizza and lock yourself in a closed room and call it a brainstorming session with your team. When you practice turning an objection into an objective, you become one with the donor – talking their language and becoming a unified front to solving the crises of the world. Well maybe!

What's the best way to turn a "no" into a "yes"?

To begin, make sure you cover all the known objections you routinely hear in your main presentation. Typically, every organization has a few objections they hear over and over. Since you know you're likely to hear those objections, deal with them head-on before the donor has a chance to mention them.

Also, when someone says "no," they typically give a reason, such as, "No. This is not in our budget for this year." If they don't give a reason, ask for one by stating, "What's making you say 'no'?"

When you know the reason behind the "no" you can combat it and turn it into a "yes."

Why do my donors keep saying "no"?

If you constantly get a "no" from donors, you need to do some more question asking—but this time of yourself. Evaluate your approach.

- Are you asking questions?
- Are you asking the *right* questions?
- Are you filling the donor's need?
- Are you personable?
- Would you give to you?

Here are some sample tie-downs you will find useful to turn the donor's 'no' into a 'yes!'

18 standard tie-downs-

Aren't they?	Don't we?	Isn't it?
Aren't you?	Shouldn't it?	Isn't that right?
Can't you?	Wouldn't it?	Didn't it?
Couldn't it?	Haven't they?	Wasn't it?
Doesn't it?	Hasn't it?	Won't they?
Don't you agree?	Hasn't she?	Won't you?

If you're not sure of your approach or how you come off to others, then ask a trusted colleague or friend and let them know you don't want a sugarcoated answer. Ask them to be brutal and give you the truth. The more you evaluate your skills and then make positive corrections, the better your fundraising results will be.

From controlling the conversation to giving "the ask" to combating objections to assessing yourself, questions are the key to success. What questions are you going to ask today?

How much research is necessary to prepare when planning to meet a potential donor?

Knowing what questions to ask depends on what answers you are seeking. Research is key when preparing your plan of attack. Did I say attack? You do not want to attack a donor. You want to play nice in the sandbox and be certain not to put foot-in-mouth. Let me explain, I have a love for horses. Each Wednesday morning I travel forty miles to my favorite farm where my horse is housed. There is a trainer who grooms and feeds her each day. I just like to ride! If you, Mr. or Mrs. Fundraiser contacted me by telephone, mail, or email and talked about your least desirable animal being a horse, I would be turned off. Whatever you said after that about your great cause would be inadmissible and I would immediately show you the door.

Do your research. Research can be done on a single individual, company, or special interest groups. If your cause is to raise funds for a special needs camp, then you want to research all of the above looking for clues to where these groups of people and businesses give their dollars. Another tip is to know where people with the same interest congregate. Do they attend a conference on a specific topic? Look to see if you can find a LinkedIn group where these people connect.

When I was working with the United States Chamber of Commerce we had a whole division dedicated specifically to researching. When the leadership team made an appointment with a leader of a fortune 100 companies, there was plenty of information to research on the company and on the executives. Before going to an appointment the team would receive a brief. They brief would contain information on the CEO's hobbies, type of dog, name of spouse, and sometimes the girlfriend or boyfriend's name. The research team was awesome! You can find some of this same information – the World Wide Web can be your friend for fundraising.

Statistics can be outdated. Is this information still worthy?

Let's clarify outdated. Do you mean 3-5 years old or older? You want to be familiar with the most current statistics available. Using statistics greater than 5 years old will not give you as much credibility as knowing current information. Here are statistics from Giving USA, American Association of Fundraising Counsel, www.aafrc.org; Grassroots Fundraising Journal, www.grassrootsfundraising.org; National Center for Charitable Statistics, www.nccsdataweb.urban.org.

2006: $295 billion in private money was given to nonprofits. (This does not include government funds or earned income.)

Where did it come from?

- 12% Foundations
- 4% Corporations
- 76% Individuals
- 8% Bequests

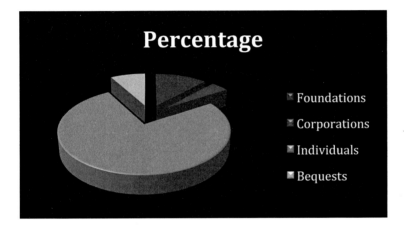

More than half of this money comes from the middle class, working class, and poor people – in other words, people like you and me give more than those with money. Could explain why they have more money in their pockets!

Here is another way to look at these statistics.

- 70% of households give
- The typical household supports 5-10 organizations annually
- The median amount contributed per household is $1,300 - $2,000 per year.

What is the income source or sources for nonprofits?

Grants	-Foundations -Corporations -Government -Service clubs -Faith-based
Individual's	-Membership -Major Gifts -Monthly giving -Benefit events -Workplace giving -Planned gifts
Earned	-Goods -Services -Publications -Investment income -Cause-related marketing

Source: Adapted from Andy Robinson, Selling Social Change (Without Selling Out): Earned Income Strategies for Nonprofits.

~Jossey-Bass, 2002

Knowing this information comes from credible sources give you some basic knowledge and will allow you to have an intelligent conversation with a potential donor. However, I suggest accepting this information as basic knowledge and applying the statistics from your local area. Your local area could be a small community, urban sprawl, the United States, or international gifts. Whatever local area means to you is where you start. Your grassroots efforts will make a difference when presenting yourself as a knowledgeable and effective fundraiser. Now how do you get the appointment? That would be effective communication 101.

*A life spent making mistakes is not only more honorable, but
more useful than a life spent doing nothing.*

~George Bernard Shaw

Chapter 3
Basic Telephone Scripts

For years I coach people in fundraising. One of the greatest fears I find is 'telephone brain freeze.' I can recall when working with the United States Chamber of Commerce, one of the telemarketers had a fear of talking on the telephone. In person he could sell you anything. Put a telephone in his hands and he froze.

An exercise to help him overcome his fear of the telephone was to set an egg timer in front of him. He had exactly the time of the egg timer to funnel through to get his point across to the person on the other end of the telephone. The timer started at 'hello.' This would often mean getting through the gatekeeper. Do you know anyone like this?

Whether you have a fear of the telephone or speaking to a potential donor face-to-face, be prepared. When you are prepared you will have greater confidence in yourself. If you are not prepared it will show-up in your conversation. One way to be prepared before picking up the telephone is to create a telephone script. The following pages provide sample scripts to use as a guide. The scripts may be changed to fit your needs and mission of your organization.

One trick I learned from my coach is when you ask a question, wait for the answer – STOP TALKING – this will take a bit of practice, because 30 seconds may seem more like 30 hours. And the first one to speak loses. If the potential donor starts to ask questions back – you're in!

What is the best way to approach a potential donor or member?

✓ Be sure you talk to the decision maker

✓ Speak effectively; make notes of their objections and concerns. Listen for any 'hidden message.'

✓ Ask for their gift/membership and then be quiet? This is extremely important. I will refer to this technique many times throughout this book.

Mistakes are the portals of discovery.

~James Joyce

Simple Approach

Good morning/afternoon Tom. This is Connie from the local Nonprofit Association. I am calling as a volunteer for the association. I have found that your business and I have benefited in many ways from the services and program of the association. [Name a sample of the services.] The organization needs our help. Can you increase your giving this year by $_____?

Close

Thank you. Your gift may be tax deductible. Do you realize this will only cost you 65 cents a day?

How should the organization list you and your business in the giving directory?

Tom, Thank you again.

Seminar Participation Commitment

Hello I'm Connie of Get to Work Nonprofit Organization, which as you no doubt know is the largest organization providing optimum services and opportunities for our members.

We will be holding a job expo, April 25, to be held at the local Hotel and Convention Center. The event will be running from 12:30 am to 5:00 pm.

We will feature a Dress for Success Fashion Show to include apparel for men and women, resume writing workshops, booth exhibits, contests, and giveaways for the attendees.

We expect approximately 1,200 attendees. You were suggested and we also feel that you are a perfect match as the top sponsor of the event.

BENEFITS

- ✓ This will get you in front of your audience
- ✓ Exposure to over 1,200 attendees
- ✓ You will be the only top sponsor of the event (provide details of sponsor benefits you are offering?)
- ✓ Many more benefits too numerous to mention over the telephone.

The reason for my call today is that I can be available as early as (day) to stop by and discuss in more detail with you! Would you like to meet in the morning or afternoon?

SPEAK WITH ENTHUSIASM!
IT'S CONTAGEOUS

Getting Through the Gatekeeper

Hello I'm Connie Pheiff and I am calling to speak to the President/Owner/decision maker of [business name.] Is he or she in? Tell him or her I'm calling about a business proposal and would like to speak to him or her.

You have several options here – some may sound simple, but they work. I know because I tested and use these techniques.

- ✓ Get to know the gatekeeper
- ✓ Set-up a meeting with the decision maker
- ✓ Ask the gatekeeper for help if the decision maker is not available
- ✓ Ask when the decision maker will be available
- ✓ Start a conversation with the gatekeeper; ask open-ended questions such as – when will the decision maker be available? I am in the area often, if I see the decision makers car I will stop by; ask what type of car the decision maker drives
- ✓ Don't be afraid to ask questions
- ✓ Don't be in a hurry to tell who you are, or why you are calling. Keep the gatekeeper intrigued.

Getting the Meeting with the Decision Maker

Hello I'm Connie of Get to Work Nonprofit Organization, which as you no doubt know is the largest organization providing optimum services and opportunities for our members.

The organization has been in existence since 1984, since that time our services are increasing to include expanded services to neighboring counties. Our services have grown to include career seminars to both men and women. While our services are increasing so is the needs in the community. With help from business leaders such as you, we have been able to increase services in most cases.

Since the beginning we recognize one basic fact, every case, every individual is different. This is why we have no set plan or preconceived ideas about how your business can help. That is why I am here, to show you how supporting the Get to Work Nonprofit Organization will have a positive impact on your business, what you should know about us, and how your support will gain additional business in the next year.

If you don't have a philanthropic plan, we can create one for you. To achieve this, we have various ways you can give.

Now, so that I can more intelligently talk about how we can work together I would like to ask you a couple of questions. (Use two or three questions...too many will end the conversation. The goal is to get the decision maker talking about his or her passion for giving.)

✓ What has been your philanthropy giving in the past year? I don't need to know the exact amount, but roughly what was your giving?

✓ Why do you give to this organization?

- ✓ How did you feel after supporting this organization?

- ✓ What other organizations would you consider supporting?

- ✓ Because of economic conditions and competition we know that today every business has concerns. What do you consider to be your three main business concerns?

- ✓ What would you like your customers to know about your business?

This is my suggestion to a solution of your business concerns. (Provide samples of your organizations newsletters; email blasts, website, or events where the company receives immediate marketing opportunities. I like to call this creative marketing).

The reason for my call today is that a member suggested you and we also feel that you are a perfect match as the top sponsor of [name the event.]

We hope you will support the Get to Work Nonprofit Organization. "I need time to consider."

Perfect, how much time do you need?

STOP AND BE QUIET…Let the donor speak first.

You can use the following telephone script during campaign season and if you are an organization with a concern with the election results. If you are not clear of your organization's political opinion and allegiance, you can always refer to Sarbanes & Oxley Act of 2002 that provides the standards for the nonprofit sector. Most 501(c)3 organizations should not participate with political pacts.

Election Pitch

It probably goes without saying that we are very concerned about the November elections. We think they are going to be critically important for small business. The Chamber's Board has me getting in touch with each of our members. To be blunt, we need some help. Do you have a moment we could talk about it?

We have a razor thin majority in both the House and Senate. Loss of just a few seats means the chairman of the Senate Labor and Human Resources Committee, and speaker of the House and other possibilities too scary to mention.

On the other side of the coin, if we can gain a few seats we can override vetoes coming out of the White House and all of a sudden we have a chance to do something real about the liability problem, over-regulation, taxes and so forth. It would certainly make living with the final two years of the current administration much easier to deal with.

We cannot allow a coalition of unions, trial lawyers, and radical environmentalists to buy the next election. The AFL-CIO alone spent more than 35 million dollars and they have committed almost twice as much for next year. Who knows how much the trial lawyers have set aside to make sure their gravy train doesn't disappear.

The Chamber is working nationwide to identify races that can go either way and that have a clear cut philosophical difference between the candidates. We are then doing everything we can to get the folks with the white hats back here to Washington where they can do some good.

The problem is simple. If we are going to do this right, it is going to be expensive. The Chamber's Board is asking each of our members to help in underwriting the cost. One nice thing about it is that your contribution is tax deductible in the same way that your dues are. This is not a PAC; we do not give money to candidates or parties. Most of our members are kicking in an amount equal to their current dues. I'm on the phone to make sure we can count on the help from the Smith Company.

Are you in?

STOP AND BE QUIET…Let for the donor speak first.

What is the best approach to the 'ask?'

I find the best approach to the 'ask' is a direct hit. Weather you are going for the 'ask' of fortune 100 company CEO's or a local mom and pop business, the best approach is not to waste anyone's time. We are all busy. We are doing more with less. When I call to schedule an appointment I let the decision maker know why I am coming. When you tell the decision maker you are calling from X association they will know immediately why you are calling. The conversation often turns into you making the 'ask' over the telephone.

Although a time saver, this is not always the best approach to asking. If you are a fundraiser in an educational institute, for example, you need to wine and dine your funders throughout the year. Touching your funders at least seven times eases the pain when the annual giving campaign begins.

Be open, direct, and touch
your funders frequently

Chapter 4
Membership Letters

On day number two after starting my work with a local Chamber, the greatest benefit for the sole-entrepreneur member was the health care benefits, ended! Health care is costly. A mom and pop organization needs assistance from organizations such as the Chamber of Commerce group association to create a program that will offset the cost of coverage. The loss of this benefit was costly to the Chamber in terms of membership loss and dollars. The following weeks and months to follow a coalition of Chamber organizations teamed up to research and create a new program.

It was nearly one-year to the date a new program was launched. Unfortunately, that came too late for many of the members who could not wait for the Chamber to get their ducks in a row. It was my job to regain the membership loss. This took some creative marketing. I started with telephone calls to members to rejoin and contacting local businesses to become a Chamber member for the first time.

The first program developed was the Chamber's Ambassador Committee. I was able to increase the six-person committee to 86 in one year. I will share the details for the program in a later book in the series. For this book we are focusing on letters and telephone scripts. If you are a membership organization the following letters will be a helpful source of information.

Invitation to Join
Simple Version

Dear Jane,

Thank you for your interest in joining the Area Chamber of Commerce. Great things are happening at the Chamber lately. We led the way on saving jobs at a local manufacturing company; the region was named one of the 10 "All-American Cities" in 20xx based in part on The Chamber managed Regional Economic Development Strategies; we earned an "Equality Award" from the Urban League.

We continue to represent the business community on the local, state, and federal levels, assist our small and growing companies, and support education and workforce programs.

Our professional development programs, networking opportunities, and free consultation through our Business Solutions Center offers your business the best "return on investment" for your membership.

Please look over the materials in this packet and call me at 570.555.5555 if you have any questions. I look forward to welcoming you as the Chamber's newest member!

Sincerely,

Invitation to Join
Simple Version

Dear John,

The mission of the Chamber of Commerce is to help businesses flourish and prosper. Thank you for your inquiry regarding membership in the Chamber of Commerce. Your business and employees can benefit from Chamber membership in many ways. Such as [list your benefits, for example]

- Discounted telephone long-distance services.
- Group health insurance plans
- Valuable business contacts through networking opportunities
- Increase you and your employees business skills by attending professional business seminars
- The Chamber will refer business to you
- Be in tune with local business issues that may affect your business by receiving the Chamber eNews Blast
- FREE airtime with local media outlets (value $1,000)

Business happens today, don't wait to take advantage of these and other member-exclusive benefits! Join the Chamber today, and let us work for you.

Sincerely,

Invitation to Join
Long Version

Dear Jane,

Thank you for your interest in the State's Convention and Visitor's Bureau membership.

I have enclosed our membership package for your consideration. Your are probably asking, "How will this membership benefit me and my business?" Honestly, many of our members were asking the same question before becoming a member of the bureau. I suggest looking at our website, contacting other bureau members, and taking a test ride by attending one, two, or three of our programs FREE.

You will learn about how our members benefit from membership. You will receive a FREE business listing on our website and publications.

After checking us out you still have questions about the benefits and services we offer, give me a call to schedule a personal visit to discuss membership.

The state is flourishing, and business is thriving and this is the perfect time to join a membership organization where every member benefits.

Membership costs $_____ and is a one-year membership from the date you join. We accept all major credit cards, cash and checks.

Like what you see – complete the enclosed membership application and return to the bureau with your investment of $_____ made payable to the State's Convention and Visitor's

Bureau or call and we can bill your credit card and start your membership benefits today. We look forward to welcoming you and your organization as new bureau members!

Welcome,

Invitation to Join
Long Version

Dear John,

Thank you for your recent request for information on membership in the Chamber of Commerce. To help you make the best decision about participating in our association, I have enclosed some information about the Chamber's mission, plan of work, member services, and benefits.

You will discover that membership in the Chamber of Commerce is an investment in the future of our community and its economic development. As a Chamber member you will also have the opportunity to help carry out the Chamber's program of work and give your business a great deal of positive exposure through networking, sponsorship, and marketing opportunities. And lets not forget about the Chamber benefits.

- Discounted telephone long-distance services.
- Group health insurance plans
- Make valuable business contacts through networking opportunities
- Increase you and your employees business skills by attending professional business seminars
- The Chamber will refer business to you

- Be in tune with local business issues that may affect your business by receiving the Chamber eNews Blast
- FREE airtime with local media outlets (value $1,000)

The Chamber's staff and volunteer ambassador's are committed to working hard on your behalf to insure the future of the local economy and quality of life. It is important to be part of a group that takes this kind of initiative to make a difference.

After taking a few minutes to review the enclosed information, John, I am confident you will like what you see. If you have any questions, please do not hesitate to call me at the Chamber office, 570.555.5555.

Sincerely,

Personality can open doors – but only character can keep them open.

~Elmer G. Letterman

Chapter 5
Membership Telephone Scripts

I have had several mentors or coaches in my life. At the time, I didn't think of these people as coaches or mentors, but looking back now, I see that they really were.

No matter where you are in your fundraising career, don't be afraid to seek out a coach[1]. Look for somebody who is a successful fundraiser—a person you admire or would want to emulate. You could also seek out a professional coach—someone you pay a fee for their coaching services. Either way, it'll be an investment in yourself you'll never regret.

I quickly learned from my coach *The Art of the 'Ask.'* Good communication is important when speaking to a donor in person, through a letter, or over the telephone. A conversation over the telephone is as important as having a face-to-face conversation. The person on the other end can read your body language, knows if you are passionate about your work, and appreciates your candor and integrity.

---

[1] You can get more information about coaching by calling 570.906.4395. Or send an email to info@conniepheiffspeaks.com.

Invitation to Join
National Member Track

Hi John, this is Connie. Thank you for taking my call. I'm calling from the National Association. I'm calling quickly – first to update you on our nationwide campaign to pass our business legislative program. Second, to ask for your support of our work on behalf of small business. Vital legislation is up for a vote in congress and will have a major impact for business.

You may have been reading about this campaign already. There are a dozen new bills designed to help small business stay profitable and competitive. It's the most important legislation in the last ten years.

The three most crucial bills are legal reform, regulatory relief, and a small business tax package. Our most important goal is to pass liability reform this year.

We have declared war on trial lawyers. We're fighting to level the playing field and end lawsuit abuse against business. Don't you agree we have to get this done?

Senate Bill 555, the Liability Reform Act features caps on punitive damages and fair share liability. It also specifically protects small businesses with less than 25 employees.

We need your support as a member. Our dues are $_____. Can we count on you too?

WAIT…WAIT FOR AN ANSWER.

Great. I'll send a statement for $_____ to your attention. Or I could save you time and a stamp by putting your dues on a credit card. Thank you!

Invitation to Join/Renew National Member Track

Hi John, this is Connie. Thank you for taking my call. I'm calling from the National Association. I'm calling quickly – first our Board of Directors has asked me to alert the business community, through our membership to legislation that will cause a dramatic increase to the overall net profit of all businesses. It's important and it'll only take a couple of minutes, if you've got it the time? Great!

- ✓ Liability reform
- ✓ Regulation reform
- ✓ Income tax reform

Are all poised for action in Congress.

To make this pending legislation law, we must elect a pro-business congress. Right now, we have a republican majority – not a pro-business one. Even though this congress is sympathetic to business interest, they are not passionate about your needs.

In the last election, there was a net loss of 145 representatives, because the head of the Unions spent $35M to buy a congress. (Pause) Right now the Unions has $60M stashed away because of the new credit cards the union has issued, so their 'war chest' for the upcoming elections is twice as big because they got an additional $12M from raising all union dues nationally.

Let's say he only does as good as he did in the last election – we lose the republican majority in congress and kiss the recently won tax relief good bye, and forget about liability, regulation, and income tax reform.

I don't know whether you're aware that the organization has a new president. The first order of business is to serve notice that we will not allow the Unions to buy through legislation what they cannot negotiate at the bargaining tables.

John, to elect a pro-business congress – we must have the financial involvement of business now. By investing $_____ to $_____ it not only gives us the necessary resources to continue shrinking the federal government; it also gives us the opportunity to meet the challenges and elect a congress favorable to your needs.

The response has been great! Ex: 80% committed $_____, 45% for the full amount. Lets cut to the chase; we need your commitment now. May we count on you too?

WAIT...WAIT FOR AN ANSWER.

When one door of happiness closes, another opens; but often we look so long at the closed door that we do not see the one, which has been opened for us.

~Helen Keller

Membership
Renewal Track

Hi Jane, this is Connie from the National Association, how are you today? Could I have a few minutes of your time to introduce myself to you as your new contact? Also, to thank you for your past support of the National Association.

Third was to inform you that the United States Senate will be going to vote shortly on the product liability and legal reform Act of 2002 and want to get your opinion on the issues.

**That's the bill that would put a cap on punitive damages for frivolous lawsuits.

I am sure you're aware of the little old lady leaving a restaurant and splashing hot coffee on herself, well most people do not realize that their sky rocketing premiums are going to pay those legal fees. We really need to tame the lawsuit abuse in this country. We are fighting the trial lawyers association on suites like this. We feel that the legal system is out of control. It is costing businesses and consumers billions of dollars per year. This has got to change.

Your membership is up for renewal shortly and we are asking our members to reinvest with us at this critical time to make sure our voice is heard and we can lobby with congress to really cut this ridiculous spending and put some of the dollars where it is needed most - In your pocket.

Last year your total investment was $_____. Can we count on $_____ investment this year?

WAIT FOR IT!

Membership
Renewal Track

Hi Jane, this is Connie from the local Chamber of Commerce. I see you have not renewed your annual membership.

After several months of invoicing and attempting to contact you we have come to the conclusion that you do not wish to renew your membership. We sincerely hope you reconsider your membership with the local Chamber of Commerce.

We count on local business to provide the community with support and feedback on important issues that businesses face each day. We offer excellent business opportunities through various programs, such as education, environmental, small business loans, and awesome networking programs sponsored by businesses such as yourself.

[Ask Questions]

- ✓ Let me ask, how many educational seminars will you pay to attend this year?
- ✓ How would you like to attend a Chamber seminar FREE?
- ✓ Did you know the Chamber offers free seminars? The topics range from labor law, business plan design, to securing an SBA loan.
- ✓ Why is the membership investment a concern?
- ✓ Why don't you consider using one of our three payment plans?

Don't let a business building opportunity pass you by. Reinstate your Chamber membership today. Don't hesitate – reinstate your Chamber membership today!

Chapter 6
Personal Touch

A good fundraiser tells everyone about the nonprofit and its mission. That means you have to approach donors—both new and established—and consistently give information about your organization. Even if someone has given money every year for the past decade, you need to keep the conversation going about the nonprofit and how it benefits the community stays top of mind.

Most people you'll be contacting have either shown an interest in the organization in the past, or they have given in some way—either money, time, or in-kind products/services. Therefore, you're technically dealing with warm contacts rather than cold ones. That alone should ease any fears, increase your confidence, and make your job easier.

What's the best way to get information to donors?

Many people in fundraising think they need a glitzy brochure and other sales materials to present to donors. In reality, your donors don't want to see that because they don't want their donated money being spent that way. If you get the brochure production donated, that's great; just make sure you clearly state that somewhere in the brochure. The same goes for any other media outlets where you may advertise, including billboards, radio and television ads, etc.

Additionally, if you're mailing that brochure or sales material, you have to pay for the postage. That alone can add up to a lot. And again, it's an expense donors don't want their money going toward.

Social media is a low-cost marketing option, but remember that the older generation hasn't embraced it as readily. So if you rely primarily on social media to get your information out there, you're missing out on a large pool of potential donors. If you don't use social media you're missing out on a large pool of potential donors. It's a double edge sword.

When it comes to spreading your information, the best approach is to have multiple balls in the air. In other words, if you know someone wants to see a brochure, then send them one. If you know someone loves social media, then connect with them there. If you know someone prefers phone calls, then pick up the phone and call them. Do what each donor likes best. I still find the best approach is the old fashioned way—face-to-face.

What's the NPO guru's secret weapon for getting the word out?

The one thing I find works best is to send a personal, handwritten note. In fact, I believe in handwritten notes above anything else. It's that personal touch that makes me stand out to donors.

I also find that picking up the phone and calling someone gets the results I want and expect. As a fundraiser, you simply cannot have call reluctance. And if you're calling warm contacts, why should you fear calling them?

If you're calling a big donor, you'll want to schedule a time to meet with them face-to-face. So you tell them that right up-front: "I want to meet with you. All I need is 10 minutes of your time." Then you meet with them. That's how you get the information to them. It's about having the confidence to pick up the phone, to be direct, and to meet them face-to-face. If you can't do that, then someone else (from another organization) will … and that person will ultimately get your money.

Face-to-Face Presentation

Hello Mr. Jones, I am Connie Pheiff from the local nonprofit organization, which you no doubt know is one of the largest community providers of programs and services. We've been around for nearly 50 years serving the general public – mostly people who have fallen on hard times. Due to economic conditions there is a greater need for our services – we know that there is a need to broaden our reach to include neighboring counties. In most cases we have been able to increase our services, but not completely. Funding the programs becomes an issue. You understand?

Since opening our doors, we recognize one basic fact; every individual and circumstances are different. This is the reason for my visit today. The need in our community is greater than ever before. We need your help.

Now, so that I can more intelligently talk about how together we can help the community I would like to ask you a couple of questions. First, your have been a donor to the organization in the past. What is your experience with the Nonprofit Organization? What are your recommendations for increasing services to those in need? How can we make that happen?

Yes, I agree the organization needs to increase community awareness of the issues. With that in mind can we count on your support again this year? We are asking our contributors to increase giving by 10% this year - can we count on you? Of course, you can increase your gift with a greater amount. We would accept your gift at any amount.

WAIT –

Thank you, I had a lovely afternoon visiting and learning about your passion for the community.

How do I behave and have an impact with the donor when meeting face-to-face?

I find that when I meet with a donor, especially one of my larger donors, the discussion goes in the direction of the donor's reasons for philanthropy giving.

People will give; they just need to be asked – and you're the right person to make the 'ask.'

Greet your donor with a warm smile, a firm handshake, and a complimentary remark of some kind - "I love your décor," "You have an impressive business." be honest about your compliment. If you are fake the donor will know it. If you are offered something to drink, TAKE IT! If you decline a beverage, you are declining their hospitality and they may decline making a donation. I do recommend not drinking alcohol, unless the host is drinking a glass of wine – then take it, sip it. Don't get sloshed.

Start off with a little small talk. Probe! The best topic is your donor. Learn more about his or her business, their hobbies, and their family. It's human nature; people like to talk about themselves. Look for a natural transition to the business at hand. One of the best conversation transitions is to ask the door – "how is business?"

- ✓ Philanthropist will give to people they know, like, and trust.
- ✓ Take control of the conversation to some extent. For example, suggest a place or seating arrangement for your meeting.
- ✓ Don't sit across from your potential donor. Sit beside them.
- ✓ Never give away your documents, you keep control of them and give at the appropriate time, such as at the end of the meeting – as leave behinds.
- ✓ Make sure you are speaking with the decision maker. If there is a spouse or business partner that needs to be part of the decision, then you may want to reschedule the meeting when you can meet with each party together. Meeting individually is a time waster.

Close

The best close is a good opening. If you probed sufficiently to find out what motivates the donor, your presentation did the 'ask' for you. Your close is simply affirming the donor's gift and completing any necessary paperwork. The best closing attitude is to assume the gift. Ask how the donor will provide the funds to close the conversation. Offer payment plans if you got 'em.

Handle any questions or objections directly and then keep going with the paperwork. If the donor says something like "I have to write a check today?" Look the donor directly in the eye and say "yes," then continue with your paperwork. Yes, a handshake is as good as gold – but I would have to say – GET IT IN WRITING!

We gain strength, courage, and confidence by each experience in which we really stop to look fear in the face…we must do that which we think we cannot.

~Eleanor Roosevelt

Chapter 7
Get Donors to Call You

New and experienced fundraisers always ask me, "How do I get donors to return my call?" The answer: Be persistent.

It's rare that a donor will call you back immediately after your first attempt. Remember, they're busy (as are you). They have a company to run, a family to take care of, social obligations to fulfill, and a life to live. Unfortunately, you and your nonprofit are seldom at the top of their list of priorities. But the more persistent you are in your follow up, the greater your chances of getting a call back.

What's the best way to build rapport with someone when I haven't even spoken to the person yet?

It's true that donors are more apt to call you back if they like you or feel a sense of connection with you. So how do you develop that before even speaking to them? One way is to leave a message about something important to the donor.

For example, I once was trying to reach a man who I knew was an avid fly fisherman. I had left several messages with no reply. About a month later I learned that a fly-fishing convention was coming to town. So I called him again and left a message stating, "Hi Jack. I called to let you know that there's a fly fishing convention coming to town. I have the details about it. Call me back and I'll fill you in."

A few hours later, he called me back. Of course, I gave him the details of the convention, and then I made my "ask" for my organization. He wrote me a check that day.

Another way is to find someone who knows the person you're trying to reach. Then when you leave a message, you can say, "Hi Monica. Lisa Peterson at the University said I should call you. She mentioned that your organization is trying to [state something you've learned they are trying to do that ties to what your organization does]. My organization has similar interests. I'd love to discuss this more with you."

Find whatever triggers you can that will create desire and interest in the other person. That's what prompts a return call.

What's a good approach for timing follow up phone calls?

No one wants to appear like a stalker, calling a donor every day. My advice is to call three times within a two-week period. If there's no reply, then let it go for a week or two. Psychologically, this makes people wonder, "Why isn't she calling me anymore?"

After that week or two break, call again, and this time relate the message to something the person has an interest in, such as, "Hi. I haven't heard from you. Did you know that X is happening in the community? You need to be a part of that. Give me a call and I can fill you in."

Follow Up Calls

Hello Gatekeeper, this is Connie calling. We spoke yesterday, and said we'd give another shot this afternoon. Is Mr. Decision Maker in and can I talk with him or her for a few minutes?

Right, I see. Look gatekeeper, you've been very helpful, and I'm in a spot where we're trying to reach a fairly large number of people tied to our Association event, quickly. Is there any way that you can put me on the gatekeeper's calendar for an official appointment? I need at most 20 minutes or so, and I'm pretty sure Mr. Gatekeeper will want the information I have for him or her. Is that something you can do for me?

WAIT…WAIT FOR AN ANSWER.

Should I leave a voicemail?

Leaving a voicemail is not my normal practice. I will make an attempt to reach the decision maker directly. If after seven attempts I still have not been able to speak directly to the decision maker I will make a decision to let this one go – or leave a voicemail. At this point leaving a voice message never hurts.

A former colleague of mine shared a story of a potential donor he just had to connect with. After seven attempts to speak directly to the individual, he chose to leave a voicemail. It went something like this…"Hello John, this is Ted. After several attempts of trying to speak with you – and failing – I decided this morning I would leave you a voicemail. It was God who led me to this decision. You see each morning when taking a shower I have a conversation with God – and he always answers my call. I figure if God, as busy as he is can return my call, then I would not think that someone in your position would be too busy to return my call. My number is 570.555.5555. Call me."

John returned the call to Ted within about twenty minutes. John is one of Ted's biggest contributors.

Is it always a phone call? Can't I just send an email?

You can certainly send an email. The problem is that most busy executives get literally hundreds of emails each day, so there's a high chance yours will get lost. Of course, if you've tried calling for months and can't get a reply, then by all means send an email.

When you do use email, try to attach an article of interest so the person sees value in opening your message. Then, you can call and say, "Hi. I thought you might like to know that [insert whatever the pertinent article topic is you're going to send]. I'm going to email you an article about it. Take a look and give me a call."

If you still don't get a reply, you can call and leave a message stating, "I sent you a great article about X. I hope you've had a chance to read it. I have some ideas about it too. Give me a call."

Do whatever you can to pique their interest. What do you know about your donor that you can use to build interest and rapport?

So, let us not be blind to our differences – but let us also direct attention to our common interests and to the means by which those differences can be resolved.

~John F. Kennedy

Chapter 8
What to Say to Donors...and What Not to Say

You received a return call from your donor (or you got through directly), you've made an appointment with them, and you've shown up (on time) at the person's office or a neutral meeting spot, like a café. Now that you have the person sitting in front of you and their full attention, what do you say? How do you get the donor to contribute?

This is your time to shine. What you say (and don't say), as well as how you guide the conversation, will determine whether you leave empty handed or with a commitment for a contribution.

What are some killer opening questions to ask?

A few of my favorite questions to ask at the beginning of a conversation with donors include:

- ✓ "Mr. Smith, when I say [insert the name of your organization], what one word comes to mind?"

- ✓ "Ms. Jones, what positive things do you see [insert the name of your organization] doing in the community?"

- ✓ "Mr. Peters, what one thing would you like to see [insert the name of your organization] do for our community?"

Questions like this are designed to get the donor's opinion and feedback, and to have them feel like they are in control of the conversation (which they really aren't—we'll get into that in a moment).

What are some questions to never ask a donor?

A common concept in coaching is that there are no dumb questions. When talking with donors, however, there are some very dumb questions that should never come out of your mouth. They include:

- "Have you ever heard of [insert the name of your organization]?" (If they say "no," then why should they support you?)

- "Tell me about your company." (You're approaching them for money, so you should know all about them already.)

- "What will it take to get you to support [insert the name of your organization]?" (This conjures up images of the old, stereotypical used car salesperson. Don't go there.)

Additionally, if you mispronounce the person's name, you're heading for trouble. With all the diversity in today's society, it can be difficult to say someone's name correctly. If you're meeting with someone who has a tricky name to say, practice saying it beforehand.

Do I need to know everything about my organization and how it operates when I talk to a donor?

You don't need to know the nuts and bolts of your nonprofit. Too often people get stuck and think they have to know every single thing about the organization, so they spend hours and hours researching but never talk to a donor.

To raise money for your cause, you don't need to know every minute detail. Sure, you need to know where the money is going, what kind of programs your nonprofit offers, what kind of results they get, how your organization impacts the community, and other surface level information. But you don't need to know how the program works minute by minute, who makes what decision day to day, and other nitty-gritty details.

You also need to know if the money given is tax deductible. There are some rules in fundraising and how taxes apply. You can find out through your state's standards program how that works in your area.

How do I stay in control of the conversation?

Remember this old sales saying: "He who asks the questions controls the conversation." In other words, you need to ask questions of your donors rather than simply tell them everything you know.

The best fundraisers ask questions—lots of them. If you go in to your meeting and spend all your time telling the other person how wonderful your organization is, that won't get you the results you want.

The key to getting the person to donate is to know what their passions are—to know what interests they have in the community and what they want to see happen. The only way to know those things is to ask.

And yes, it's okay to ask personal questions … as long as you phrase them correctly. For example, suppose you're raising money for an organization that supports cancer research and you've heard through the grapevine that the person you're talking with recently lost their father to cancer. Since it's not pubic knowledge, don't say, "Isn't it true that your dad died of cancer?" That's tacky and obtrusive. Rather, you could ask, "Do you know someone who has had cancer?" The person will likely reveal the personal connection.

If the person you're talking with has a personal story that's been featured in the news, it's okay to relate that to your cause. For example, if you're raising money for a cause that fights drunk driving, and the person you're talking with was featured in the news because their son died as a result of a drunk driver, you could say, "We understand that you are fighting to rid the roads of drunk drivers. That's exactly what our organization does. Can we count on your support?"

The key is to use your questions to lead the conversation and ultimately the donor to a "yes" reply. What questions are you going to ask at your next donor meeting?

Glory lies in the attempt to reach ones goal
and not in reaching it.

~Mahatma Gandhi

Chapter 9
Go for The 'Ask'

All fundraising ultimately comes down to "the ask," which is nothing more than you asking the donor for what you want. If you never ask, you'll never get. But you don't want to risk asking at the wrong time. You need to do your "ask" at the right moment, and in the right way.

What is the best time to do "the ask" when speaking with a donor?

Even though "the ask" is akin to "the close" in sales, you don't want to wait until the end of your conversation to bring it up. In fact, the best time to ask is at the beginning of the meeting. In other words, start at the end.

Of course, if you're doing an event where you're hosting a dinner, typically at the end of the meal someone comes up to speak and asks everyone to break out their checkbook. That's fine for that venue.

When you're talking one-on-one with a donor, especially a CEO who doesn't have a lot of time and who knows why you're meeting, you don't want to waste time. Often, the person can only spare 10 to 15 minutes with you, so you better ask right up front or you may miss your chance.

What's the best way to phrase "the ask"?

All questions to your donor, especially your "ask" question, should be open-ended. In other words, don't ask a question that prompts a "yes" or "no" reply. So rather than ask, "Will you give $10,000 this year?" ask, "How much are you giving this year?"

This approach has two benefits:
1. You're "assuming the sale" and not giving the person a chance to say "no."

2. You're not pre-selecting how much the person will give. If you ask for a dollar figure, and the person was actually thinking about giving more, he or she may think your figure is all you need so that's all they'll give. In this case, you could get less than what the person was planning. That's called leaving money on the table.

It takes practice to be direct, but donors at higher levels will respect you more when you are.

Of course, they may reply with questions for you, such as:
- "What value is the community getting from my money?"

- "What is your organization doing differently this year?"

- "How, specifically, is my money being spent?"

This is when you go into the details of what your cause does—after "the ask." You can talk about how many people your organization has helped, specific programs you're offering, success rates for your programs, etc.

What signals do you look for to get commitment from the donor?

When you're talking face-to-face with a donor, always look at the person's body language, as that often gives away more about what the person is thinking than their words.

Are they acting distracted (doodling, tapping their fingers, looking at their phone), like they'd rather not be there? Is their body "closed" to you (arms crossed)? Or are they engaged and making eye contact? Are they leaning in to talk with you? Reading body language is a skill that you need to practice. After all, someone could have their arms crossed because the room is cold. So look at the whole picture, not just one element, and read all the cues around you to determine how the meeting is really going.

Don't be afraid to be direct with your 'ask.' Remember the 'ole saying, "Ask and ye shall receive." Who are you going to 'ask' today?

Chapter 10
Fundraising Letters

When you are fundraising the same rules apply when letter writing. You need to make your 'ask,' make your case, show the benefits, and stop talking.

Philanthropy giving is not decreasing; your strategies just look different. Donors receive dozens of fundraising letters – how will your letter stand out? Think outside the box. What can you do to be different?

Credibility, consistency, and personal touch

Writing a letter is nice; it creates awareness of your mission and vision. Imagine you are the CEO of a major corporation; you receive dozens of fundraising letters in the mail. Which organization do you support? Do you even open the letter? Or do you file them in the trash? Think about it, how will you stand out from the others?

I have shared with you some of my personal strategies such as finding out where your donors gather, personal notes, share a local story, and become their advocate. When I was starting out in the business of fundraising I was often tongue-tied. In my small community there were four large corporations I wanted to make the 'ask.' I had to get the inside scoop on the leadership team. I was failing to get meetings with the decision makers. I learned company picnics were part of the employee programs at each company. Ah I had an idea! What do you serve at picnics - watermelon? I purchased four watermelons, typed a note on a large shipping label, attached to the watermelon and personally delivered to the decision maker's office. At two locations I left the melon with the gatekeeper (had no other choice). Of the four, I received callbacks from three, and secured a business donation from two of the companies, and created an employee-giving program with the third. All in all I would say it was worth the price of the watermelon.

The following pages provide fundraising letter samples, if you choose to go this route.

Fundraising 'ask' Letter
Simple Version

Dear John,

You are a member of a very special group – a graduate of Smart Leadership School! And we need your help. As a graduate of the class of 2012, you know firsthand how valuable our programs are to the participants and to the community. Over 10,000 people have graduated from our programs and are working in various ways to improve our community. As we approach our 20th year of operation, we continue to seek new ways to reach even more people. One of this year's class projects is a pilot leadership program for high school students. We are also researching new programs that will serve other segments of the local community.

In order to realize our mission, we must raise a substantial portion of our budget through individual contributions. Our Annual Alumni Appeal has begun and we are on our way to reaching our goal of $100,000 for Alumni Giving. Your contribution will help fund scholarships, alumni events, publications, and training materials for our students. In the near future you should receive a follow-up phone call from another graduate as part of our Annual Phonathon.

You will be able to make your pledge to the school, a 501(c)3 (nonprofit) organization, on the phone or you may use the enclosed pledge card and envelope to send your tax-deductible gift now. All pledges are payable by June 30, 20xx the end of our fiscal year.

We appreciate your past support and hope you will seriously consider a gift this year to help ensure that the programs reach more people and continue to strengthen our community.

Fundraising 'ask' Letter
Long Version

Dear John,

On behalf of the Arts Fund Board of Directors and the 40 arts and cultural organizations that participant in the united campaign. I personally thank you in advance for your time. You're *ABC Fuel Oil Company* is a loyal supporter of the arts in our area over the past several years. As you know this has a tremendous impact in our community. This brings me to the reason for my contacting you today.

In 2000, the first united campaign for the arts raised $230,000. Last year, we topped the million-dollar mark for the first time. Over the past 13 years, participation in the arts such as yours has helped the fund raise over $6 million for the arts in our region. Such investments have encouraged the arts to grow and flourish.

Such investments, benefits the important work of the arts and cultural organizations in Pennsylvania, and thus enhances the quality of life of the entire region. A thriving arts community with significant offerings is critical in making our region a great place to live and work and raise a family.

The arts play a pivotal role for our families and our children. Recent studies have documented that children who have the opportunity to study music and art actually test higher in academic areas – especially science and math. Your investment supports numerous programs to encourage children to enjoy the arts including:

> ➤ The local symphony's series of concerts for children
> ➤ The art Museum's "VanGo' that brings art to area schools and children
> ➤ Local Players Theatre with a focus on children between the ages of two to ten
> ➤ Acting classes at the local community theater
> ➤ Art lessons at the Arts Center School and Gallery
> ➤ Art in the Park
> ➤ Dance training with the Youth Ballet
> ➤ Friends of Jazz – Jazzmobile for children

In addition, the opportunity to participate in the arts offers our children, especially our teenagers, positive alternatives as opposed to less attractive things that they can be doing with their time.

Your support of the arts has a significant economic impact on the region. Although I hope everyone supports and enjoys the arts because of the arts' human spiritual and aesthetic value – the ability of art to make us pause and reflect. It is also worthy to reflect on the vital role that the arts play in our economy. The National Association of the Arts Fund recently completed a study that documents that for every $1 a community invests in the arts, $4 is returned to the community. That sounds like a smart investment.

Your investment in the arts helps you - Attracts and retain a more creative, diverse, and qualified work force. Providing cultural and vibrant programs is important for employers to be able to keep their good employees here locally.

We need art in the community to inspire creativity in all aspects of an individual's life. In order to succeed in today's economy, we need people who can color outside the lines and a vibrant arts community encourages that kind of creative thinking.

In addition, your investment is an efficient and effective way to support the arts. One of the reasons business leaders created the fund was because they were tired of spending so much staff time and resources to review grant requests from dozens of arts organizations. Thus, they created the Arts Fund as the federated fund for the arts and cultural organizations. In turn, each organization that participates in the united campaign for the arts agrees to forego some of their own fundraising efforts to support the united campaign.

Finally, your generous support of the arts is recognized in the community throughout the year. Every donor of $300 or more is listed in the Arts Fund Contributor's list that is published over 100,000 tied for arts audiences throughout Pennsylvania. For donors of $3,000 or more: as a major donor, your investment will be acknowledged on the first page of this highly publicized and well-read list.

Within the next several days, I will contact you to arrange a brief meeting to discuss *ABC Fuel Oil Company's* participation in this year's campaign. Thank you for your investment in the arts of our community.

Sincerely,

Is there such thing as writing a lengthy letter?

Yes, did you grasp the long version of the fundraising letter? Can you tell me what's wrong with this letter? Put yourself in the shoes of the potential donor, what's wrong with this approach? It's too long…you lost me at hello. It is only natural to want to spill your guts, tell the donor the cause, benefits, and effect of his or her donation. Lets be honest, do you read every piece of mail you receive knowing it's a solicitation letter? Another cause is asking for money. I would guess the answer is "no."

The best approach is a simple one or two paragraph letter. Consider using a post-card. On the front of the postcard list several bullets where you communicate the benefits to the potential donor for supporting your organization.

Chapter 11
Fundraising Telephone Track

Another form of fundraising is phonathon's. This is common among educational institutions. If a phonathon is one source of fundraising, you will have preparation. First, you will need to solicit your volunteers. These individuals may have a passion for your mission, but do they have the skill to pick up the telephone and make the 'ask' on behalf of your organization? In addition to ordering lots of refreshments, you will need to create a phone script and train your volunteers.

I was leading a Chamber membership campaign once upon a time. I recruited my volunteers, ordered refreshments, and I created a packet of information that included

- ✓ An overview of the Chamber
- ✓ A listing of the programs and services
- ✓ Member benefits and programs
- ✓ Committees, etc.
- ✓ Current member listing
- ✓ Board of Directors

I thought my training was detailed enough for the volunteers to be comfortable to dial for dollars. It came time for the phonathon to begin and the volunteers just sat there...what are they waiting for I thought to myself. Finally, one of the volunteers asked for the script. Script...why do you need a script.

My assumption was wrong. Just because I spent hours creating the colorful information document, it did not provide the volunteers the 'words' they needed. I again was assuming these are professionals; I should not have to tell them what to say on the telephone...they should know how to ask for money. Wrong! When you are working with volunteers you need to spell out exactly how you want them to behave, including what to say to potential donors. Without missing a beat, I put together a telephone script for my volunteers.

Fundraising Telephone Track

Hello, may I speak to _____?

This is Connie, a volunteer for the local Chamber. I wanted to remind you about our summer cocktail party on the docks to be held on Friday, June 20, 20xx, from 6-8:30 pm. A presentation will be made to Representative Smith for his outstanding community leadership at about 6:45 pm. Will you be joining us? It's always a great time!

While I have you on the phone I would like to verify your work and home addresses and phone numbers? Do you have an email address?

Today a group of volunteers, including myself are helping the Chamber with their Annual Appeal to raise $10,000. The funds will support youth programs and member activities. You should have recently received a letter describing the purpose of the Annual Appeal. Do you recall receiving this letter?

With membership dues covering only 60% of the program costs, the need for member support becomes increasingly important. We're asking each member to raise $500 for the Annual Appeal. I have made my commitment/pledge today and invite you to join me in the effort. Because the Chamber is a non-profit organization, your contribution is tax-deductible.

We have a special incentive this year. If your contribution is $50 or more and we receive your payment within ten days of this call, your name will be entered into a drawing for a $50 gift certificate to Bistro Bistro. There's even a second chance drawing. If we receive your payment within 30 days of this call, your name will be entered into a drawing for a $25 gift certificate to another area restaurant of your choice.

If previous donor-
Thank you for supporting us in the past.

If previous gift was $50 or more, ask for $100-
Can we count on your commitment or pledge of $100 at this time? (STOP! Don't speak until they do.)

If previous gift was less than $50, ask for $50-
Can we count on your commitment of $50 or more to help us reach our goal? (STOP! Don't speak until they do.)

If not a previous donor, ask for $50-
Can we count on your commitment of $50 or more to help us reach our goal? (STOP! Don't speak until they do.)

If asked what the money is used for-
Contributions are part of our operating budget and are used to maintain our professional, high quality programs. As a nonprofit organization, we need to keep programs affordable for small companies and individuals. These funds also support the schol-

arship fund, minority scholarships, and training materials for our youth.

If yes-
That's terrific (super, wonderful, etc.)! [Name], your pledge is really appreciated. We'll send you a note confirming your pledge with a return envelope. Remember to return your check within 20 days to be eligible for the drawing. Otherwise, we'll need to receive payment by the end of our fiscal year, June 30th. We are all proud to be part of the Chamber and hope you will continue to support it both with your time and money.

If undecided
Is there another amount that would be better for you now?

If no-
May I send you a pledge card and return envelope for your future consideration?

Closing-
It's been great talking to you. I also wanted to let you know that membership applications are available at the Chamber office. Please recommend a local business for Chamber membership.

Thank you for your consideration.

When developing a phonathon, breakdown your contact list by region, business categories, and alphabetically. Be sure to include as much information as available about the potential donor. This will take research – contact your local college for an intern who can do the research for you.

Allow your volunteers to select the names of people and businesses they know. They will be more comfortable making a warm call than a cold call.

Chapter 12
Did you say – Sponsorship?

Another opportunity to raise funds for your organization is to pursue sponsorships. I have worked with organizations that use the term 'sponsorship' to raise funds. A true sponsorship is a business or individual giving money for something in return, such as marketing, tickets to an event, or a orchestrated meeting with a VIP, etc. It is up to you and your organization to determine what is in it for the sponsor. Another term for exchange of goods and services is in-kind. In-kind gifts typically come from the media outlets; radio, television, billboards, newspaper, etc. Your organization will determine the culture and proper lingo for sponsorships. My goal is to provide you an example of sponsorship letters.

One event that will seek sponsorships is an organization that honors leaders in the community. The Girl Scouts will honor women of distinction. This event brings in potential new donors. These are people with a relationship or allegiance to the honoree. If you select this type of events it is important the honoree understands his or her responsibilities.

The most important of these is inviting, making a personal contact, and soliciting friends, family, and acquaintances to support the program by attending and giving to the event on their behalf. Giving has the potential of becoming a sponsorship. As a fundraiser it is your responsibility to make this happen. When you receive the honorees guest list, this gives you permission to contact the individuals. This becomes a warm contact.

Generic Event Sponsorship Letter

It is with great admiration that the Girl Scouts honors Ms. Jones with the 2010 Woman of Distinction award.

Ms. Jones has recognized you as a community leader that understands the needs of Girl Scouts. Would you consider sponsoring this event to help us secure our programs for the future of our girls? Programs where there are opportunities for the girls to build self-confidence, character, and learn life skills while having fun.

Our needs continue throughout the year, and we count on the generosity of people such as you. With your corporate support the Girl scouts can continue to serve the girls in the region.

We hope to see you at the event and again, thank you for your support.

Yours in Girl Scouting

You need to keep your eyes and ears open for funding opportunities. A local business was instrumental in hiring legal immigrants. Nearly 90% of the employees were Hispanic. I saw an opportunity. The Girl Scouts have Hispanic girls wanting to be part of the Council programs and we have a local business employing their families. This was an opportunity to 'ask' a local business to sponsor specific programs for Latino girls and enhance the employee benefits. Perfect win-win combination!

Specific Program Sponsorship Letter

Dear John,

Thank you for your time and meeting with me recently. I enjoyed sharing information with you about Girl Scouts and how we might partner with your business to reach out to the Latina girls in the region with our program.

The number of Latino residents in the region continues to grow. These families are especially interested in having their children participate in positive youth activities. Today's youth especially girls, need adult support and guidance to discover who they are, to develop their interests and to reach their full potential. Additionally, research shows girls need a safe environment, both physically and emotionally to accomplish this.

Girl Scout councils have a long and successful history of partnering to enhance learning opportunities for girls. For 93 years Girl Scouting has been the world's preeminent organization dedicated to girls where in an accepting and nurturing environment girls build character and skills for success in the real world. In partnership with trained adult volunteers, girls develop qualities that will serve them all their lives like leadership, strong values, social conscience, and conviction about their own self-worth.

I am enclosing a proposal, which outlines a key initiative the Council is planning for our new membership year. The project is specifically designed to reach out to the families and ultimately other Latino families in the area. Going forward we believe this project will serve as a model for other community outreach programs in our council service area. We are asking you for your public and financial support of this program.

I am happy to meet with you to discuss this initiative further or to answer questions you may have. I will follow-up with you in two weeks on the sponsorship proposal.

Sincerely,

Pg. 2 - Sponsorship Proposal

Our Mission – Girl Scouting builds girls of confidence, courage, and character who make the world a better place.

Project Title – Latino Community Outreach

Project Overview – The Girl Scouts will recruit at least five adult leaders to deliver the Girl Scout Program to the Latina girls registered during the recruiting Scout day, and to serve other girls joining the Girl Scouts from the area. The trained leaders will establish age level troops and deliver the Girl Scout program through troop and group activities, special family programs, and council sponsored activities. The Council will provide program and leader material in both English and Spanish for girls and leaders. We will also provide training and support services for all adults volunteering to work with these girls. The Latina girls will have access to special grants, which will provide financial assistance to defray the normal cost of membership and participating Girl Scout programs and activities.

Transportation will be provided to enable the girls to attend troop activities and council sponsored programs.

Project Components

> **Adult Leaders**

> Part time staff: The Girl Scouts will hire one bi-lingual community outreach coordinator to over-see a troop of Latina girls, develop programs for the Latino community in the area and recruit new girl members and bilingual adult volunteers. The coordinator will serve as the initial contact for the Latina troops and once adult volunteers are trained the coordinator will support the adult volunteer leaders with their troops.

> **Sponsorship**: $15,600

> **Assumption**: Coordinator works 20 hours per week at an hourly rate of $15.

> **Special Annual Scholarships**

> Initial membership: this scholarship will help pay the annual membership fee, full year's troup dues, uniform and handbook for each girl.

> **Sponsorship**: $6,000

> **Assumption**: 30 girls at $200 each as follows
> - $10 annual membership fee
> - $52 troop dues
> - $13 handbook
> - $125 for 3 uniform pieces

➢ **On-going Membership**

This sponsorship will help pay the annual membership fee, full year's troop dues, and handbook for each girl on an on-going basis.

Sponsorship: $2,250

Assumption: 30 girls at $75 each as follows
- $10 annual membership fee
- $52 troop dues
- $13 handbook

➢ **Camperships**

This grant will provide an additional $200 per girl to offset the cost of one resident camp summer session. Girls can choose from more than 40 summer camp programs to learn about the out-of-doors and to develop strong citizenship qualities. A camp brochure is enclosed.

Sponsorship: $6,000

Assumption: 30 girls at $200 each

➢ **Program**

This sponsorship would enable each Latina girl to attend up to five council sponsored programs during the year. Council sponsored programs may include: Gym and Swim, Healthy Habits, Health Living, Science Discovery, CSI: Forensics, and From Stress to Success. Please see the enclosed Table of Contents from the current program book for a list of other Council sponsored programs.

Sponsorship: $3,000

Assumption: 30 girls attend 5 programs each at an average cost of $20 per program.

➢ **Service Unit Events**

Adult leaders will work with the girls to plan service unit events including but not limited to

- Family Day Camps
- Cinco de Mayo Celebrations
- Mom and Me Days
- Dads, Uncles, Grandfathers, and Someone Special Dances

Sponsorship: $3,000

Assumption: 30 girls bring 3 guests to one event at a cost of $25 per person.

➢ **Transportation Sponsorship**

The Council will provide transportation for girls from one or more central location to and from troop events at schools or the factory.

Cost: $5,700

Assumption: Round trip transportation for 30 girls to and from troop activities and to and from five Council sponsored programs during one year.

➢ **Staff Training**

The Girl Scouts will hire an instructor to teach conversational Spanish to all staff members working in communities with Latino populations.

Cost: $1,500

Assumption: Five staff members attend 20 hours of training at a cost of $15 an hour for the instructor and materials.

Total Sponsorship: $45,550.00

Enclosures: Camp Brochure
Current Year Program Book

Specific Event Sponsorship Letter

Dear Jane,

So many wonderful things has resulted from the National Association community partnerships. New volunteers have stepped forward, from local to national; people offered their time and talent bringing new program resources which enrich the sessions at our youth summer camps last summer and our current Association sponsored events; and we raised much needed funding support for the Association programs.

We want to thank NoName Bank for your past support as a media sponsor. This year we would like to invite NoName Bank to increase that support and become a major sponsor of one of our current events. Major sponsorship of these events is described in the attached proposal.

At the Association, one in every eight of our community youth participates in one of our programs – that is one better than the national average. This is a tribute to the dedication and creativity of our volunteers. As we work to bring the opportunities of the Association program to every youth who wants to attend our programs, our need for human, financial, and in-kind resources grows. Our initiatives is vital in helping us raise new funds, to keeping our communities involved and informed about the Association programs and for uncovering resources that will help to keep our programs strong and relevant.

This event is very important to the association. We are funded through a combination of special grants, program fees, fundraising, sponsored events, and United Way dollars which, although a faithful source of support, has been steadily declining over the past several years and now represents only 12.5% of our annual budget. Since September alone, we have given $110,532 in financial aid to 3331 youth participants to help them with the cost of their membership fee, handbooks, and program material. We receive new requests for assistance daily.

This year we are particularly proud that income from two of our money earning programs accounted for nearly 50% of our operating budget.

With NoName Bank help, we can make sure that every youth in the region knows that he or she will have a place in one of our programs. Attached is a brief outline of the proposal for sponsorship. Please do not hesitate to call if you have any questions and I would be happy to meet with you at your convenience.

Thank you in advance for your support of the National Association.

Sincerely,

/enclosure: Sponsorship Proposal

For-profit organizations generally have a line item for sponsorships and project underwriting separate from their donation line item. Be clear when making your 'ask.

Chapter 13
Sponsorship Telephone Track

The previous chapter provided different examples of sponsorship letters. The letters may be an introduction, or a follow up to a previous meeting. Either way you will need a sponsorship telephone script prepared when making your call.

Sponsorship Telephone Track

Hello, may I speak to John?

This is Connie, of the National Association. I am a member of the Association.

Today we are calling our members to let everyone know that the Association will be hosting our Annual Cocktail Event, May 6 at the local Smith Hotel & Convention Center. This year we are adding a fundraising component with a silent auction. Registration and inspection of items to be auctioned will begin at 5:30 pm, followed by music, hors d'oeuvres, and cocktails.

Hundreds of local businesses and individuals donate items…tools, vacation trips, clothing, dinners, savings bonds, artwork, hair styling televisions, etc. Cash donations are also accepted to cover the food cost for the volunteers. Sponsorship opportunities are available to (develop sponsor opportunities that echoes your organization.) Be creative and choose your own special item. Your donation will not go unnoticed.

As a sponsor of this event you will receive-

> A featured article in the Association Newsletter (circulation 270,000 Quarterly)

> Ad in the event program book

> Signage at the event

> Marketing in the Association promotional material pre and post event

> Banner ad on the Association website

I'd also like to verify your work address, telephone number and fax? Do you have an email address? [I suggest you have a separate work sheet available to receive the updated contact information.]

We're asking each member to contribute an item or cash donation of $25 or more to this event. I have made my commitment today and invite you to join me in the effort. Because the National Association is a nonprofit organization, your contribution is **tax-deductible**.

> *It's easy to donate*

Can we count on your commitment for an auction item of $25 or more to help us?
[STOP! Don't speak until they do.]

If asked what the money is going to be used for

Contributions are part of our operating budget and are used to maintain our professional, high quality programs for our members. As a nonprofit organization we need to keep our programs affordable for small business and individuals.

If yes

That's terrific (super, wonderful, etc.!) John, your $_____ donated sponsorship item is really appreciated.

We'll send you a note confirming your pledge and form to fill out describing your gift. If you are giving a gift for the auction such as a gift certificate, it must be signed and be sure to include any special restrictions or time limits.

Do you have a preference to how you would like your gift to be acknowledged?

The deadline for receiving your sponsorship is May 20. [If providing an auction item] What is the best time for an Association volunteer to pick up your donated item?

If unsure: For drop off or pick up of your item please call the Association at 570.555.5555 and ask for Connie to make arrangements.

If Undecided

Can I help you in selecting an appropriate item or sponsorship gift?

If no

May I send you a pledge card and return envelope for your future consideration?

May I send you an invitation to attend the cocktail event? The cost for the evening's event will be $30 per person. This is a new event that gives an opportunity for the Association to bring together its members and guests in a social setting with a purpose **TO HAVE FUN.**

Everyone loves a fun night out, everyone loves good food, and everyone will go home with a bargain or with something they just couldn't live without. We are all proud to be part of the National Association and hope you will continue to support it both with your time and money.

Closing

[Confirmation of sponsorship and/or auction item.] It's been great talking with you today. Do you recommend anyone else that would like to sponsor or donate an item or someone that would like to attend the cocktail event?

Thank you for your time and consideration.

Volunteers enjoy helping and supporting the organization. The tip – 'ask.' If you don't ask, you will not receive.

Chapter 14
Get your Board on Board!

For any nonprofit, people are the organization's most precious resource. When the wrong people are taking on the fundraising role, the results can be damaging to the organization. Having your best and brightest do "the ask" is great, but you also need an individual with the right attitude and passion. Then everyone wins.

Now, let's face reality. An organization with successful campaigns can say they have a robust staff, each person with independent responsibilities and a focus on an area of expertise. But we know that the nonprofit sector is not always so fortunate. All too often, nonprofits must rely on committed volunteers and board members to work on the fundraising initiatives. Add in the Pareto Principle (or the 80/20 rule) where you have 20% of the people doing 80% of the work, and you can see how difficult it can be for organizations (and individual fundraisers) to thrive.

In fact, in many nonprofits, it's common for a staff member to wear the hat of multiple positions. For example, I was once hired as the executive director for a local United Way. My background is that of fundraising and leadership. Before long I learned the board had a different plan for me: they also wanted me to be the bookkeeper. I quickly expressed my concerns, because bookkeeping is not one of my strengths. But because of funding, the board could not hire a bookkeeper, so it became me. And I admit it...bookkeeping is not something I enjoy or look forward to doing every day. So I strongly recommend that if you are wearing multiple hats, be sure all those hats consist of a job you know and are capable of doing. Otherwise you will go bonkers!

Know Your Team

Fundraising efforts have multiple individuals involved, including:

> ➤ The executive director (CEO). In addition to oversight of the mission and programs, the executive director has the responsibility of being the "face of the community." If the executive director is not seen or known in the community, then he or she should be replaced immediately.

> ➤ Development officer. According to *The Nonprofit Times* (2011), the mean salary of a good development officer commands $65,000. Unless you are an organization that has the financial ability to hire at this level, the executive director, a part-time development officer, or a volunteer will be leading the fundraising initiative. A good development officer will have good writing and verbal communication skills.

> ➤ All staff members. The person leading the fundraising needs to keep the staff up-to-date on the initiatives. Why? Because *everyone in the organization is responsible for fundraising*. Without fundraising, there are no funds for payroll and no staff to deliver programs. This is a joint effort, period!

➢ Committed volunteers. You will be able to find volunteers who are committed to the mission of the organization. For example, my mother teaches sewing and design. She is also a cancer survivor. Each year since her recovery she holds a fashion show with her students. The proceeds of the show go directly to the American Cancer Society. Do you think the students' families are willing to pay to see their loved ones in a fashion show? Of course! Do you think the American Cancer Society praises Mom for her hard work of putting together the fundraising program without asking for help? Most definitely! Mom has a passion for the mission of the American Cancer Society. You can find people just like Mom in your community.

When you find volunteers, keep them fired up so they build excitement for the organization, which encourages others to join. When I was working with a local Chamber of Commerce office, I started with 6 volunteer ambassadors and grew the group to 86 people. We worked hard together—and played hard together. That excitement, energy, and camaraderie attracted similar people to get involved.

➢ Membership. Not all nonprofit organizations have membership. You may! The Girl Scouts are a membership organization. My work with the Girl Scouts involved the Green Hat Society. This is a group of adult Girl Scouts who are still dedicated to the mission. The development of this group led to endowments.

➢ Board of Directors. Most, I repeat, most board members join because they believe in your mission. It needs to be strongly stated in the board agreement that the number one responsibility of a board member is to give, get, or get off. (Many organizations forget this little detail!) Of course, I have seen organizations go overboard by stating an amount a board member must give annually ... or get off. I was on one of those boards, and before they could tell me to get off, I resigned! The lesson: Never tell someone how much to give. What if they want to give more?

Be sure you are recognizing your board for their work. Board members are volunteers who often have full-time jobs, family, and other outside interests. Board members and committed volunteers are there to support the organization; you need to support them. Recognition goes a long way. Remember, honey is sweeter than vinegar!

➢ Outside coach (if you are able to pay, I recommend). If you select to hire a coach, it is important the paid staff understand how to surrender control. Yes, this has been an issue. A coach can help you design the fundraising plan, address board concerns, lead board retreats and training of the plan, and create grassroots efforts where the organization and board can work together toward a successful goal. Coaching will develop the executive director into a successful engine for the organization. You can find a coach that will write grants, develop the marketing plan, and handle direct mailings, individual solicitations, and board retreats. For more ideas go to www.idealist.org.

When you hire an outside coach, be aware of the legal matters that surround this type of worker. This is not an employee, and if you treat the person as one you will find yourself in legal trouble.

Get Your Board Involved

I can't express enough the importance of board participation. Each board member should be a cheerleader in your corner who lets the community know your nonprofit is the go-to organization for philanthropy giving.

There is no limit to your board's participation and fundraising efforts. However, keep in mind that these are volunteers and they may have different interests or time constraints. Right from the get-go, make sure your board members are on board (pun intended!). Ask them to help with planning and executing the fundraising plan.

For example, perhaps your board members enjoy a good party. If so, ask them to plan a special event, host a house party, or initiate a giving program in their workplace. Other ways the board can be involved include representing the organization in the community, providing names of philanthropists, "asking" for dollars, doing personal letter writing, and personally thanking the donors for their financial and volunteer contributions.

If you have ever been on a board, then you know the constant cry for help board members hear from fundraisers. Now that you are on the other side of the table you need to be cognizant of when enough is enough. This is one of the reasons why board members should have term limitations. I worked with organizations with no limitations, and it was chaos! Board limitations need to be addressed and clearly labeled in the by-laws.

Too often, individuals join a board and have no idea how to best contribute to the cause. Help your board members determine their strengths. The person could be so committed that he or she will do whatever it takes to move the organization forward. But he or she needs your help to determine what that something could be. You live this work day in and day out while the volunteer helps a day or two per month. When your board members see where they fit, they will be more engaged and motivated.

Grant Din, the executive director of Asian Neighborhood Design (www.andnet.org) in San Francisco, has created a great board set up. As he explained, "We have one board member who's a development director at another nonprofit, which is perfect, because he can emphasize the importance of fundraising and not have others tune him out the way they might if a paid staff member said the same thing. We also have another board member who has really pushed for full participation by the board, and the two of them have created more of a giving and getting environment."

Your board members need to feel wanted and appreciated for their hard work. Happy board members mean results!

Also, be sure your board members understand the mission of the organization. Just because an individual becomes a board member, do not assume they know all there is to know about your organization.

When new board members join, take some time for show and tell. This does not mean you have an orientation for each new board member. Instead, select a time of year, typically at the beginning of the fiscal calendar, where you induct new board members. Following the induction, ask seasoned board members to lead a program to educate the new members and allow time for questions and answers. You can create colorful pie charts to explain the financials, and a PowerPoint presentation to explain the program's mission and work of the organization. Let them know the significance of the organization and all the hard work you do for the community. When board members feel your passion, they will exude that passion to the community … and dollars will follow.

Make it easy for your board members to give to the organization. When your board gives, it makes it easier for them to ask others to give to your organization. Provide your board with choices and list opportunities to give, such as

Board of Directors Annual Appeal
Ways to Give

Name _____   Date _____

(Please use name you wish to appear in all publicity and recognition)

As financial stewards of the organization, it is important for every Board member to make a financial commitment to support the organization. Any monetary contribution to the following events and/or campaigns can be considered as your board contribution.

Please note that designations through employee United Way campaigns cannot be included. Gifts of your time as a volunteer at some events are much appreciated, but also cannot be considered part of your financial gift.

January, February, March	Board Meeting – Board Appeal
April	Council Meeting – Board Appeal
May	LPGA Sponsorship
June	Gift-In-Kind from Wish List
July	Donation for Camp Program
August	Donation for Special Program
September	Board Meeting – Board Appeal
October	Annual Organizational Meeting
November	Board Meeting – Board Appeal
December	Donor Thank-a-thon phone calls

Payment information:
(Please check your preferred option):

_____My check is enclosed, payable to:
            The National Association

_____Charge my
Visa/MC#_____

Exp. Date_____Amount $_____
_____ Contact me about making my annual contribu-
            tion through stock.
_____ My Company will match my gift.
_____ Billing Option – multiple payments

Payment Plan:

❏   Send a reminder of my annual pledge
❏   Bill me monthly
❏   Bill me quarterly
❏   Bill me annually
❏   Do not send a reminder of my annual pledge

Volunteers are Priceless!

Who are your volunteers and where do they come from? Your volunteers will come from all walks of life. Corporations often have programs where employees are encouraged to volunteer in the community. Students need to give X number of community hours for class credit if they are looking to be submitted into college or the National Honor Society. Retirees want to contribute to society and continue to be a huge pool of potential volunteers. Criminals re-entering society need to do community service. You can research organizations in your community that work with these programs, such as The Salvation Army and The MacAuley Center, Chamber of Commerce, etc.

Also, contact local organizations, including high schools and colleges with leadership programs, to let them know you have volunteer opportunities available. If you have the financial resources you can contact the Area on Aging and hire a part-time senior aide. You will put a smile on a person's face when you give them a sense of purpose.

Just as we discussed board training, we also need to address volunteer training and getting a commitment. When you develop a formal process for volunteer training and explain the mission and programs of the organization, you will make the volunteers' experience more comfortable—for you and the volunteers. Know each volunteer's strengths and use his or her talents accordingly. If they are willing to work in the fundraising office and do not like to make "the ask," you can have them write thank-you notes or enter data into the donation software system (be sure to set parameters of how to enter the information; otherwise you could end up with duplications and misinformation.)

Volunteers need to be treated the same as staff members. When a volunteer is working on your time, policies and procedures must be followed. I had to fire volunteers on several occasions. One of the firings caused such a mess with the organization that we had to get an attorney involved. The volunteer just refused to leave. Your volunteers are the face of the organization. If you have a volunteer bad mouthing the organization or you, get to the bottom of the issue right away. If you don't deal with the issue head-on, it will only fester and get worse.

Of course, have fun with your volunteers. Help your board give, get, or get off by providing them giving opportunities.

Your board's primary function is to raise money for your organization. The board's fundraising responsibilities need to be clearly addressed in your organization's bylaws.

Don't be afraid to use the "give, get, or get-off" approach.

Chapter 15
Sponsorship Examples

Golf Tournament Sponsorship

Secure the highest prestige by teaming with the National Association to promote your organization at our Annual Golf Tournament. Partner with an organization that fosters positive youth development, community service, and volunteer commitment.

Two days filled with golf clinics, buffet lunch, mobile bar, buffet dinner, and awards provide networking opportunities for golfers, guests, and clients.

Date: Monday, September 22 & Tuesday, September 23
Location: Saw Grass Country Club, Florida
Estimated attendance: 125-150
Contact: Event Planner at 570.555.5555

Presenting Sponsor at $50,000

This elite sponsorship is limited to one company

This event will be referred to as the National Association Annual Golf Tournament presented by "(name of presenting sponsor.)"

Sponsor benefits:

- Recognition as the Presenting Sponsor in all radio and television public service announcements, all news releases and print media announcements promoting the event
- Recognition as the Presenting Sponsor on the event invitations and signage
- Recognition as the Presenting Sponsor on each golf cart
- Having your organizations' name and logo identified on the National Associations website- "x" hits per day
- Recognition in our tri-annual publication

  ➢ National distribution

  ➢ Circulation 990,000

  ➢ Half page, inside front cover announcement

- Having a foursome participate in the tournament, lunch, and dinner buffets
- Providing marketing items with your organization's logo that will be distributed to each participant

Dinner Sponsor at $25,000

One dinner sponsorship is available

Sponsor benefits:

- Recognition as the dinner sponsor
- Tournament signage

- Having a foursome participate in the tournament, lunch, and dinner buffets
- Signage at the 18th hole recognizing your company as the dinner sponsor
- Providing marketing items with your company's logo that will be distributed to participants

Lunch Sponsor at $15,000

One lunch sponsorship is available.

Sponsor benefits:

- Recognition as the luncheon sponsor
- Tournament signage
- Having two players participate in the tournament, lunch, and dinner buffets
- Signage at the 1st hole recognizing company as luncheon sponsor
- Providing marketing items with your company's logo that will be distributed to participants

Gift Bag Sponsor at $10,000

One gift bag sponsorship is available.

Sponsor Benefits:

- Company logo on gift bag given to each participant
- Tournament signage
- Having two players participate in the tournament, lunch, dinner buffets
- Providing marketing items with your company's logo that will be distributed to participants

Golf Clinic Sponsor at $8,500

Two clinic sponsorships are available.

Sponsor benefits:

- Recognition as a clinic sponsor
- Tournament signage
- Having two players participate in the tournament, lunch, and dinner buffets
- Providing marketing items with your company's logo that will be distributed to participants

Awards Sponsor at $5,000

Two award sponsorships are available.

Sponsor benefits:

- Signage on the holes where the awards are applicable
- Signage includes company name and logo
- Having two players participate in the tournament, lunch, and dinner buffets
- Providing marketing items with your company's logo that will be distributed to participants

Booth Sponsor at $2,500

Twelve booth sponsorships are available

Sponsor benefits:

- One table and two chairs on a designated hole for your employees to provide brochures to market your company
- Tournament signage
- Two seats for lunch and dinner buffets
- Providing marketing items with your company's logo that will be distributed to participants

Sponsorship Commitment

Please accept this sponsorship form as evidence of our commitment to the National Association

Company_____

Authorized Representative _____

Title_____

Address _____

City_____ State_____ Zip_____

Phone _____ Fax_____

Email _____

Sponsor Level_____ Sponsor Amt $_____

Method of Payment (check one)

_____Check _____Cash _____Credit Card

Credit Card Number _____ Exp. Date _____

Signature_____

One Time Payment _____
Please attach check payable to the National Association

Installment Payment _____
Please include first payment of 50% of sponsor amount - include with sponsorship form. Second payment of 50% balance due within 90 days of event.

Return completed sponsorship
form along with your contribution to:

National Association
555 Main Street
Washington DC 20002

Thank you!

Don't sell them...ask them!

Chapter 16
Pledge Reminder/Overdue Letter

Pledge Reminder

Dear John,

Thank you for your pledge to the National Association. Your support is very much appreciated.

This is your 2012 pledge fulfillment reminder

Pledge payment due: $_____ Outstanding

Method of Payment (check one)

_____Check   _____Cash   _____Credit Card

Credit Card Number _____ Exp. Date _____

Name on Credit Card _____

Signature_____

Thank you for your prompt remittance.
All gifts are tax deductible in accordance to the law.

Increase the power of your gift! If you work for a company that matches gifts to the National Association, you may be able to double, even triple, the power of your gift. Check with your personnel office for a Matching Gift Form and send the completed form along with your gift.

THANK YOU!

Pledge Overdue Letter

Dear Jane,

It has been awhile since you attended one of our programs. We know that you were inspired at that time to make a pledge of support to the National Association, and we thank you for that.

The National Association continues to change the lives of youth in your area. Whether it is building a new cabin at summer camp, learning about what it is like to own a business, identifying the stars in the night sky, exploring new places, or collecting food for the hungry, the values and skills gained from these experiences remain with these children forever. Your continued support will improve these opportunities and make them available to even more children.

We hope that you will fulfill this pledge so that our programs reach every child everywhere.

Thank you for your support and for your interest in the National Association.

Sincerely,

It's important to include your nonprofit disclaimer on all fundraising material. Check with your state's nonprofit standards for details on the standard language.

Chapter 17
Stay the Course

Rejection hurts, and giving up is all too easy. When someone says "no" to you, even after you employ the key questions and tactics, you have to stay the course. You have to hang in there. Remember, a "no" doesn't always mean "no."

If you immediately quit after someone says "no," that means you don't believe in what you're doing. And if you're going to quit that easily when somebody says no, then that means you're in the wrong field. You shouldn't be doing fundraising.

The general rule of fundraising is that most donors give after the seventh attempt. That means they've said "no" seven times before saying "yes." Therefore, you have to ask at least seven times before someone responds favorably. Additionally, when the donor sees that you're hanging in there and are persistent, you'll win them over.

Is there ever a point when you have to throw in the towel?

Of course, you may get to a point when a donor says, "I told you 'no' and that's it!" In this case, you may want to pull back for now, but still follow up with them next year.

Or, you could nicely say, "Apparently this is not a good time for you. When would you like me to come back to discuss this?" If they get nasty and yell out, "Never!" then that's your cue to leave. It's not worth the fight anymore. But usually, when you're nice and showing consideration for them, they'll tell you to come back next month, next quarter, or next year.

But I really believe in my nonprofit's mission. How can I get people to see what I see?

If someone keeps rejecting you and you truly believe in your heart that this is the perfect match for your donor to help the community, you could say, "Mr. Redding, I must be doing something wrong because you continue to reject me. I believe that my organization is the best, and we offer the best value to help underprivileged children in the community [or whatever your nonprofit does]. Can you help me better understand how we can best help the community [or provide value back into the community]? What would *you* like to see us do?"

When you use this approach, you're going back to them, putting the ownership on them, and allowing them to make decisions. By considering their input, you're increasing their ego. And by asking and not telling, you're showing them you have a very strong belief and commitment to your organization and to what it does for the community.

Of course, if the person still doesn't see what you see, and if the person is getting agitated by your presence, it may be time to back off—at least for now.

Ultimately, your level of commitment and perseverance is directly related to your belief in your organization. How strong is your belief?

Chapter 18
The 4 Biggest Mistakes a Fundraiser Makes

We all make mistakes. There's no shame in that. But are you learning from your mistakes? Are you picking yourself up and changing course so you don't make the same mistake again?

When it comes to fundraising, there are four main mistakes I see fundraisers make. Beware of them, and how to fix them, so they don't derail your efforts or your career.

Mistake #1: Getting into fundraising for the wrong reasons.

If you don't love what you do, if you don't have a passion for the organization you're working for, your success is going to be a long and hard road. Unfortunately, I've seen some people get into fundraising because they view it as just another sales job.

I can sell anything, they think. You may be a great salesperson, but if you don't truly believe in the organization's mission, you'll have a hard time getting people to give to your cause. Plain and simple!

Mistake #2: Not realizing that you're attitude controls your success in fundraising.

Are you genuinely happy to be doing what you do? Do you believe in yourself and your organization? Do you view the world in a positive or negative light? Your answers to these types of questions will determine your attitude, and your attitude determines your success.

The people you speak to every day, whether via phone or in person, can pick up on your true attitude, regardless of the actual words you use. You know this is true, because you do it to others too. For example, you've likely gone into a retail store to purchase something and have had to interact with salespeople who'd rather not be there that day. Even if the salesperson answers all your questions and rings up your transaction quickly, you can sense if the person cares or is just there to collect a paycheck.

Your donors can sense the same thing in you! So make sure your attitude is one that donors will want to interact with.

Mistake #3: Continually blaming other people or events for your failures.

It's very easy (and very tempting) to blame others for our failures. But at the end of the day, the only thing that really determines your success is you.

Blaming others is nothing more than excuse making. How many times have you heard someone say (or have you said), "I didn't bring in any money today because…

- …I didn't have a new brochure to give out."
- …my contact didn't give me a proper referral."
- …the economy is really bad."

- …I heard that people aren't giving what they used to."

The list of excuses and blaming is endless.

Here's the truth: If you're in the right job and have the right attitude, there's no need to blame anyone or anything else. You can fundraise without a brochure, without a proper referral, and without a booming economy. Fundraisers still bring in the big money; you just have to approach it wisely.

Mistake #4: Trying to sell the organization rather than getting people to give to the organization.

Always remember that you're raising money, not selling cars or some other tangible item. So you can't "sell" the organization. Your role is to show donors the value your organization brings to the community. People give money when they believe in your cause. You gain that belief by asking questions, uncovering their passions, and showing how the organization aligns with the person's interests. Attitude and passion are what generate funds, not fancy salesmanship.

$$\text{Attitude} + \text{Passion} = \text{Results}$$
$$(A + P = R)$$

You can overcome your approach...
It takes a little
practice...practice...practice!

Chapter 19
Make Yourself Stand Out

Chances are the donors you're approaching are also being approached by fundraisers from other nonprofits. After all, the other organizations have the same database you do. Whether you're a small community organization or a national one, how do you set yourself apart?

Since any organization only has a certain percentage of their funds earmarked for philanthropic causes, you need to stand out in their eyes. In fact, when they think about which nonprofit to support, you want them to think of you and your organization first. It's a tall order, indeed, but it can be done!

How do I stand out from all the other people and nonprofits doing fundraising?

In order to stand out, you need to focus on three key things: Credibility, Consistency, and Follow Up.

- When you're **credible**, people believe that you'll do what you say you'll do. They see you as someone of your word and are eager to do business with you. You develop credibility by being honest, trustworthy, and transparent—you don't hide details and you "tell it like it is" in a tactful way.

- To be **consistent** means that the image you put out is the real you 100% of the time. You're not putting out the image of a business professional and then dancing on the tables at the bars on the weekends. Of course, a lack of consistency doesn't have to be that extreme. Someone once paid me a great compliment. They said, "You make every person you meet feel like the greatest person in the world and your best friend." Now realize that I'm not a "hugger" or overly-friendly. But when I run into people on the street, I stop and chat with them. I ask how they are (without asking for a contribution). In other words, I consistently work on the relationship even when I'm not formally meeting with them. By being consistent like this, I develop strong relationships with donors, making it easier to ask them for the dollars later on. They know that I care about them and not just their money.

- We've talked about **follow up** in chapter seven, but it's worth mentioning again. You can't just talk with your donors when you're asking for their donation. You want to make sure you're following up with them and "touching" them throughout the year. For example, if they're getting honored for something, try to attend the ceremony. If you learned that they just had a baby, send a congratulations card. If you saw them written up in the newspaper (for something positive), write a note telling them how great it was to read about their project or initiative or whatever the article was about. Follow up shows that you're aware of what they're doing and taking an interest in them.

How do I create a personal brand for myself?

The best fundraisers not only stand out, but they also have a personal brand. Just as corporations and nonprofits each have a brand, people have brands too. It's what they're known for and how they present themselves to the community.

For example, when my donors think of me, they immediately think of someone who is prepared, who has character, and who has a passion for life. That's part of my brand—what I'm known for. When someone meets with me, they know that I've done my research. I already know whether the person I'm meeting has a passion for the organization I'm representing. Whether through actual research or good questioning during casual meetings and networking functions, I am prepared and ready to ask for the funding.

The key to creating a personal brand is to figure out how you can present yourself better than other fundraisers. Often, this means stepping up your game and becoming a better communicator. It's about being excited about what you're doing. It's about asking good questions to learn about the person you're meeting.

So what can you do that's different or exceptional to set yourself apart? What can you become known for in your niche? Being like everyone else is the not the key to success; rather, it's about setting yourself apart and being known for something great.

I know it's difficult to gather the courage to break from the pack. For many years of my life, I always felt like a square peg trying to fit into a round hole. I never felt like I fit, although I tried very hard to, and I struggled with that. It was only when I gave myself permission to embrace who I was—to be confident being the one doing things differently—that I started seeing what was possible.

You want to be that one person who stands out—who has a compelling brand. When you can do that, donors will welcome you with open arms.

What's the guru's secret to really standing out?

I've mentioned this before, but my favorite way to stand out is to send people handwritten notes. Let me say it again: handwritten notes…handwritten notes…handwritten notes. Did I mention handwritten notes? But this is only the cherry on top. Before sending the note I become the NPO guru by owning my brand, by having credibility to fundraise with ethics, and by bringing value to the donors. In other words, I live by the advice I outline in this book, and I personally do everything I recommend that you do.

When it comes time to send the handwritten notes, I have something personalized and meaningful to write in each, and I actually write them myself. This will take time, but it's worth every minute. I know there are services out there that will send cards on your behalf and they make the font appear like handwriting. I'm not comfortable with that because you never know what the end product looks like. Plus, even though the font resembles handwriting, it's not my handwriting. People receiving the card still know it's a computer font. That's why I prefer the good, old-fashioned handwritten note.

You can buy blank thank you cards at any discount store or card shop. Or you can opt for custom cards that have your name printed on them. You can even use stationery in lieu of a card. It's up to you. The key is actually writing out the note yourself, in longhand. That's what really makes you stand out.

Apparently, I'm not the only successful fundraiser that employs this technique. One of my past neighbors ran one of the biggest foundations in the country. Every morning I would see him on his back porch reading the newspaper. I'd often say "hi" and on occasion even ask if he'd like to join me for coffee or a morning run (since we were both up so early), and he always replied "no." He said that he needed to spend this early morning time reading the paper.

Eventually, I asked him why he was so committed to reading the paper each day. He said, "I read the obituaries. I read the announcements to see who had a baby, who got married, who is being honored, and even who is ill. Every single one of those people gets a handwritten card from me. I've been doing this every day for many years, and this is why my foundation has one of the biggest giving dollars in the country—because I touch them every day."

I admit, I don't go to the extreme he does, but I do believe in the power of handwritten notes and attribute the practice of sending them to my success. So take some time to look through your donor contacts today. Are they all seeing you as someone credible, consistent, and dedicated to follow up? Are they receiving handwritten notes from you? Who are you going to send a card to today? How are you going to truly stand out from the crowd?

Associate yourself with people of good quality, for it is better to be alone than in bad company.

~Booker T. Washington

Tips

- ➤ People will give; they just need to be asked – and you could be the right person to make the 'ask.'

- ➤ Be genuine.

- ➤ Don't be afraid to be direct with your 'ask.'

- ➤ Breakdown your contacts by region, business categories, and alphabetically. Allow your volunteers to select names of people they know.

- ➤ Know what your asking for – sponsorships or underwriting.

- ➤ 'Ask' – if you don't ask – you don't receive.

- ➤ Get your board on board – it's their responsibility to raise funds. Make sure this is covered in your bylaws and board agreement.

- ➤ Don't sell them…ask them!

- ➤ Use the proper language for your disclaimer.

- ➤ Overcome your ole 'ask' beliefs and learn new ones.

Recommended Reading & Resources

Here is my list of recommended books and resources for you to investigate. Most of the books listed can be purchased through my website, www.conniepheiffspeaks.com.

Books

Three Feet from Gold: Turn Your Obstacles into Opportunities
~Sharon L. Lechter CPA & Greg S. Reid

438 Days to the Work You Love: Preparing for the New Normal
~Dan Miller

Crucial Conversations: Tools for Talking When the Stakes are High
~Kerry Patterson, Joseph Grenny, Ron McMillan, and Al Switzler

Crucial Confrontations: Tools for Resolving Broken Promises, Violated Expectations, and Bad Behavior
~Kerry Patterson, Joseph Grenny, Ron McMillan, and Al Switzler

The Tipping Point: How Little Things Can Make a Big Difference
~Malcolm Gladwell

Reaching the Peak Performance Zone: How to Motivate Yourself and Others to Excel
~Gerald Kushel

Beyond Fundraising: New Strategies for Nonprofit Innovation and Investment
~Kay Sprinkel Grace

The Wisdom of the Flying Pig: Guidance and Inspiration for Managers and Leaders
~Jack Hayhow

Donor Centered Fundraising: How to Hold Onto Your Donors and Raise Much More Money
~Penelope Burk

Resources

Association of Fundraising Professionals
www.afpnet.org

Foundation Center
www.foundationcenter.org

Guidestar
www.guidestar.org

Grant Smart
www.grantsmart.org

Fundraising for Dummies
http://www.dummies.com/how-to/content/fundraising-for-dummies-cheat-sheet.html

About the Author

Beginning as a student of hard knocks, Connie Pheiff was labeled as a 'rebel' always working against 'status quo.' After years of working in the nonprofit sector, Connie turned her fascination with people into a career as a successful professional speaker on business and inspiration and coaches women entrepreneurs on how to be successful. When she began her work in the nonprofit sector working with the United States Chamber of Commerce she quickly moved to the Girl Scouts and the United Way in the position of CEO. After earning a solid reputation in this sector, Connie made a profound realization. In order to achieve her dreams and passion she knew whe had to start her own business.

The Northeast Business Journal calls Connie feisty, funny, and frivolous. She has been named one of *50 Women on the Rise;* and is founder of *The Magic of Mentors* and the *Executive Women's Network*. Connie is also a columnist for the Northeast Pennsylvania Business Journal.

Connie is the author of:

> ➤ The author of *For a Long Time I Hurt Inside, But Not No More and Poem for Stefanie* (poetry)
>
> ➤ *Breaking the Glass Ceiling*
>
> ➤ *Find your Passion for Action (pocket)*
>
> ➤ *Art of the Ask...Get Into Your Fundraising Groove*

> ➤ *The Art of the Ask...A Collection of Letters and Telephone Scripts.*

> ➤ Multiple print articles across the United States

Pheiff has been interviewed on numerous radio programs, including the Marty Wolff *Business Builder Show,* Joel Boggess *Finding Your Voice, and* Oscar Bimbong *The Platform*, UK Radio.

Hailed by clients as "impressive," "outstanding," and "an exceptional leader with humor" for her no-nonsense strategies of guiding entrepreneurs to look at their business strategies differently. Connie believes the American dream is still possible - it just looks different. Connie helps women to become effective leaders and inspire change.

Pheiff continues to contribute to the nonprofit sector. Through her work the Nonprofit Sector has seen increase in revenue by million of dollars. She is currently involved in the growth and development of women through her charitable work with *Dress for Success.*

She does not stop there. Pheiff also provides workshops and programs for the *Foundation Center* with offices in Atlanta, New York City, San Francisco, Cleveland, and District of Columbia.

In the pursuit of her interest in the development of human potential, since 2006 she has studied human behavior in business and politics in the global market, and applications with nationally known groups. She also studied, and is proficient in personality analysis using the DISC$^{©}$ assessment tool and is a Master Certified Coach.

AUTHOR'S CREDENTIALS

- ➢ Master of Public Administration and Management from University of Phoenix
- ➢ Bachelor Organizational Innovation from University of Phoenix
- ➢ 48 Days Certified DISC^{tm} Instructor
- ➢ 48 Days Certified Workshop Facilitator
- ➢ 48 Days Master Certified Coach

Pheiff is listed in a number of Who's Who publications and is represented by several nationally known speaking agencies.

Connie Pheiff is married to her partner in life and business, Jeff Pheiff. This isn't their first time to the rodeo. They have a combined family that includes five children that keeps them busy traveling for holidays, birthdays, and special occasions: Stefanie Batyko Prudente (North Carolina), Michael Batyko (Pennsylvania), Jessica Pheiff Roseblade (Lake Tahoe, California), Jeff A. Pheiff (Germany) and Julie Pheiff (Virginia). They also have two adorable teacup poodles – Trinity and Mattie.

Looking for a Dynamic and Inspirational Speaker?

Call Connie Pheiff!

Her most requested keynote topics are:

- If It Were Not for Other People…Time to Take Charge of Your Life
- The UNinvited
- Molds are for Jell-O
- A + P = R (Attitude + Passion = Results)

**Contact Connie for more information at
570.906.4395
info@conniepheiffspeaks.com**

Looking for a Business Coach who will help you find the work you love?

Connie is your #1 specialist for nonprofit and entrepreneurial coaching programs.

**Contact Connie for more information at
570.906.4395
info@conniepheiffspeaks.co**

What Other's Are Saying

"Connie provides a dynamic fund development workshop to American Red Cross Chapter Leadership that was engaging, thought provoking and inspiring! Connie's expert knowledge provides answers and a call to action for board leadership. We were impressed with her preparation, program and pleasing personality! Excellent A+++++"

~Cindy Garren, Major Gifts Officer
The American Red Cross

"When Connie Pheiff speaks … her audience listens and learns! Connie was a popular speaker at the Called Woman Conference 2013 and what a story she has to share. It is the best kind of story of all—one with a surprise ending that will encourage and inspire you to discover your calling, overcome obstacles, and live with passion. Connie's presentation sparkles and shines with her wit and powerful story. She is going to change your life"

~Lynne Watts, President/CEO
The Called Woman Conference Atlanta, Georgia

"Connie was willing to share her expertise in her field to help us build exemplary assignments together. Her ability to communicate, collaborate, and contribute affected all members of the team in a positive way. I can honestly say she is one of a kind and I would be proud to work with her in any capacity. I am lucky to have worked with her and have had the opportunity to learn from her amazing skill set."

~Shawna Foster
The University of Phoenix

"I have had the pleasure of working with Connie ... she is always early with her submissions and puts forth great effort in the team environment. Connie has some intriguing viewpoints on the public administration system that I have enjoyed reading and discussing with her. She is a dedicated, diligent, and hardworking woman of substance, with quality and effective leadership skills. I am really proud to recommend her."

~Sesan Popoola
University of Phoenix

"Connie is highly recommended for her facilitation skills and expertise in people management."

~Mary Jane Saras, VP Development,
Creative Energy Options

"Connie had to deal with quickly changing work environments and mergers. She used her skills to bring her team and our volunteers through the changes without adversely affecting the program."

~Linda Szoke, Director of Sales
Split Rock Resort & Golf Club

"Connie has a wealth of organizational management skills and the ability to transfer her knowledge to the benefit of clients."

~Catherine Shafer, President
cds creative, inc.

"Connie has proven to be an outstanding leader through turbulent times and considerable change."
~Joseph Angelella, Senior VP
First Liberty Bank & Trust

"Connie has demonstrated impressive organizational skills. We raised over $100,000 in one week and brought in new members. We couldn't have done it without her help. Throughout my travels, often the first comment made is one complimenting Connie's talents and professionalism."
~Lonnie Taylor, Senior Vice President
U.S. Chamber of Commerce

"Connie has exhibited great skill and polish in marketing to business leaders, piquing interest, and closing the sales. She is skilled in the full range of marketing, negotiation, closing, follow-up, and documentation."
~Jerry Lisman, VP, Marketing
Mabis Healthcare, Inc.

"Connie is a leader in the not-for-profit arena. Her strengths involve extensive experience with strategic planning, organizational development, and motivation."
~Laura Novakowski, Co-Founder
Positive Power Strategies, Inc., 720 Thinking

"Connie delivered a flawless presentation of wit and wisdom with an entertaining twist. I highly recommend her presentation when you are looking to inspire all audiences."
~Mari Potis, VP of Events
Scranton Chamber of Commerce

The Art of the Ask: A collection of Letters and telephone scripts - is one of several books by Connie S. Pheiff. Subsequent books include Connie's life experiences from leading nonprofit organizations to becoming a leading inspirational speaker and coach for women entrepreneurs.

To be notified when additional books are published, please visit www.conniepheiffspeaks.com and sign up for alerts.

Visit www.conniepheiffspeaks.com for more speaking and coaching information

25044876R00081

Made in the USA
Middletown, DE
15 October 2015